Gh
of
Bedfordshire

Betty Puttick

COUNTRYSIDE BOOKS

NEWBURY, BERKSHIRE

COUNTRYSIDE BOOKS
3 Catherine Road
Newbury, Berkshire

ISBN 1 85306 386 X

Cover illustration by Colin Doggett
Designed by Mon Mohan

Produced through MRM Associates Ltd., Reading
Printed by J.W. Arrowsmith Ltd., Bristol

Be kind to ghosts if you should run into one,
or one should run into you. Remember, there but for
the grace of God goes you, or someone you know.

Hans Holtzer

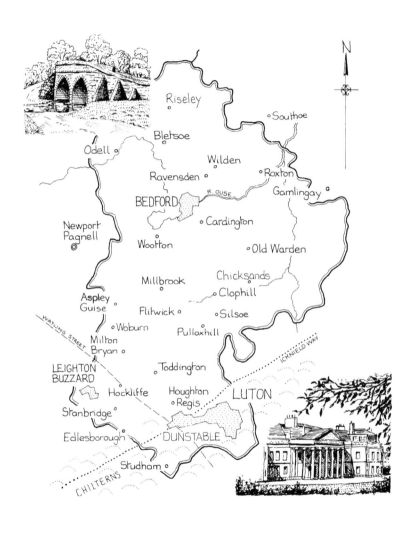

N

Riseley

Southoe

Bletsoe

Odell

Wilden

Ravensden

Roxton

BEDFORD

R. OUSE

Gamlingay

Newport
Pagnell

Cardington

Wootton

Old Warden

Millbrook

Chicksands

Clophill

Aspley
Guise

Flitwick

Silsoe

WATLING STREET

Woburn

Pulloxhill

Milton
Bryan

ICKNIELD WAY

Toddington

LEIGHTON
BUZZARD

LUTON

Hockliffe

Houghton
Regis

Stanbridge

Edlesborough

DUNSTABLE

Studham

CHILTERNS

Contents

Acknowledgements

Thank you to all the people who took time and trouble to help me, and to the staff of many Bedfordshire libraries, especially Bedford Central Library Reference Department. Special thanks to Jennie Clarke, Ruth Large, Jill Egerton, Wesley Downes, and Richard Morgan; and to Tony Broughall, who generously shared some of his own ghost-hunting discoveries with me.

Introduction

OVER the last three years I have been writing books about ghosts – ghosts of Hertfordshire, ghosts of Buckinghamshire, and now ghosts of Bedfordshire. And my strongest impression about ghosts is their infinite variety.

Some seem no more than a kind of faded old photograph. Perhaps that is why there are so many grey ladies – over the years all the colour has drained out of them. Some repeatedly re-enact a dramatic happening of long ago – a battle, a murder – or just quietly follow a route they walked in life. These too seem to be a sort of shadowy replay, and it is as if the bemused witness has tuned into what someone once called 'the cinema of time'. And some are no more than disembodied footsteps or a 'cold spot', like an invisible cube of icy space.

Others seem to be earthbound spirits, lost, unhappy souls tied by some powerful emotion such as hate, anger or even jealous love to a world they should have left behind. And some are people we love, who either at the time of death or later pay us a fleeting visit to say 'Don't worry, I'm still here.'

That is not to say that there are not evil, harmful entities, or mischievous, destructive poltergeists, perhaps the most mysterious phenomenon of all.

If or when we experience a brush with the supernatural, we realise how little we know about any of its aspects. The idea that a phantom is some creepy white apparition drifting through an old stately home at midnight is not entirely without foundation, but a ghost is just as likely to look like you or me or to pop up in a council house or modern factory in broad daylight. A wailing banshee inspires alarm, but many ghosts are more inclined to show a rather irritating sense of humour, hiding possessions, switching off lights or even trying out typewriters and photocopiers.

Bedfordshire has spectral nuns and monks, witches and highwaymen, and, more unusually, a strange little blue man. Was he an alien or someone from the fairy world? Then there are a couple of mysterious housekeepers, haunted statues, a poltergeist, a phantom hitchhiker, black magic in a derelict churchyard, and some very haunted pubs! Bedfordshire has all these and more.

But this is nothing unusual. Interest in the supernatural has never been stronger, and everybody likes a good ghost story, whether they believe in it or not. However many haunted houses and mysterious happenings I discover, the supply never dries up. As the poet Longfellow wrote: 'The spirit world around this world of sense floats like an atmosphere, and everywhere wafts through these earthly mists and vapours dense a vital breath of more ethereal air.'

I hope you will enjoy the book – sleep well!

Betty Puttick
Autumn 1996

1

The Ghost with the Rose Perfume

THE guest settled down cosily, ready for a good night's sleep. The hotel had all the charm and comfort of an old country manor house, which in fact it used to be, and being set well back from the road, it was so peaceful. He was relaxing in that happy state between sleeping and waking, when suddenly he was startled as something heavy landed on the bed near his feet.

Had he been dreaming? There was nothing there. He tried to settle down again, but then, although it was quite dark, he could just see that now there was someone sitting at the end of the bed. Alarmed, he called out 'Who are you?' but there was no response from the shadowy figure.

He switched on the light to find himself alone. Whoever or whatever had disturbed him had gone as silently as it had come, and for the rest of the night he lay awake, afraid to switch off the light. As he said afterwards, he didn't want to believe that his unexpected visitor had been a ghost, but there seemed to be no other explanation.

Shortly afterwards Lydia Dawson, the duty manageress at Flitwick Manor, spent the night in the hotel, and woke to find someone standing at the end of her bed. It was a little old lady with grey hair, wearing what appeared to be a long Victorian dress and a small white cap. She was agitated and looked as if she was crying, and Lydia thought she was trying to say something to her, but there was no sound.

Lydia leapt out of bed and ran out onto the landing. When she ventured back into her room after a little while, she found that the ghost had gone, but that the light was now on.

Towards the end of 1994, builders were engaged in renovation work at Flitwick Manor, and while working on the roof they uncovered the entrance to a little attic room which the present general manager, Sonia Banks, had not known was there. While they were working on other bedrooms the builders used the attic room to store furniture, and it was after this that the staff at the Manor realised that they had an increasingly active ghost on the premises.

'When she started haunting the hotel, I wondered if it was because we had found her little room,' Sonia Banks told me; 'so I wrote her a little note and said "Dear Housekeeper, I am sorry you are so upset, but please don't go away." I signed it and put it on the chair in the room where she mainly seems to be. I always know when she's there as the cushions in that chair show an impression, as if someone has been sitting there.'

One night Mrs Banks too woke to find a weight on her feet. She had moved her pillow so that she could lie flat, and told herself it must be the pillow she could feel, but on another occasion she woke and had the impression that someone was leaning over her.

'I have heard her walk across the floor above and slam a door when I knew I was alone in the hotel,' said Sonia, who obviously has a protective, affectionate feeling towards the ghost and wouldn't dream of having her exorcised, although at times she seems quite mischievous. 'One night I was standing in the hall talking to some visitors when the lights went out, and everyone cried "Oh!" I said "It's just the ghost" and switched them on again. But off they went again, and I kept switching them on, and they kept going off, until I said "Will you please stop it!" The visitors asked who I was talking to, and I explained that I was talking to the ghost.'

Playing with the lights seems to be a favourite activity of Flitwick's ghost, as although the lights are turned off at night, they are often found on in the morning, and sometimes locked doors have mysteriously been unlocked even when no one has touched them.

The ghost's bedroom visitations usually seem to take place around 1 am and the chef, Duncan Poyser, told me that once when he stayed overnight he too woke to find a heavy weight on his legs. 'I couldn't move and I couldn't turn over,' he said, 'but I didn't see anything.'

At first the ghost seemed to confine herself to the bedrooms, but recently she has been seen downstairs. 'We had a wedding reception here not long ago', recalled Sonia Banks, 'and they had a keyboard player to provide the music. He asked if we had a ghost here, and when we said yes, he said "I think I've just seen her." Apparently, as he was playing he looked round and saw her going out of the french doors into the garden. We asked him just what he had seen, and he described her precisely.

'On another day a lady visitor was sitting in the hall, and she too, asked me if we had a ghost. I admitted that we had, and she said "Well, she's just gone into that room." I had just locked the door of this room which opens off the hall, so I looked through a crack in the door and the ghost had put the lights on! She plays with the lights a lot.'

One of the nicest stories about Flitwick Manor's ghost is that when she is around there is a scent of roses. But who is she?

The Brooks family owned Flitwick Manor from the end of the 18th century but the first members of the family to live there were John Thomas Brooks and his wife Mary, who moved into the Manor after their marriage in 1816 and spent the rest of their lives there. They had three sons, and one much-loved daughter, Mary Ann. They were a close and affectionate family, and John Thomas, who became the High Sheriff of Bedfordshire, obviously enjoyed the life of a Victorian country squire.

When I visited the Manor just before Christmas 1995, it was decorated with greenery, scarlet candles, and tall, sparkling Christmas trees, with huge log fires blazing in the hearths. Although there have been changes in the layout of the Manor in more recent times, the lovely antique furniture and family portraits make it easy to imagine oneself back in the days described so fully in John Thomas Brooks's diary. This diary, edited by Richard Morgan and published by the Bedfordshire Historical Record Society in 1987, gives an absorbing account of a family life totally remote from that of today.

Social life – entertaining and exchanging visits – occupied much of the family's time, with occasional highlights such as balls and parties where John Thomas recorded that he 'danced all evening', and 'felt very lightsome', his mood perhaps not unrelated to various pretty young lady partners. After one such occasion he sent white camellias, violets and chimonanthus for a particular Victorian charmer to wear in her hair, which was 'so dark and beautiful'.

His devotion to his 'dearest wife, Mary' is so apparent, however, that one suspects his innocent pleasure in 'the presence of youth and beauty' gave her no misgivings.

John Thomas was very generous to many friends with gifts from the magnificent variety of fruit and flowers grown in his glasshouses, and parties of visitors were always arriving to be conducted round the gardens which were his pride and joy. He recorded many of his own visits to other gardens and horticultural shows and was obviously a keen and knowledgeable gardener.

They were a devout family, attending the nearby church twice on Sundays, and birthday presents always seemed to consist of religious works of some kind. So I felt pleased on his wife Mary's behalf to see that from one of his visits to London, John Thomas brought back some silk stockings for her.

The family's great tragedy was the death of the daughter, Mary Ann, at the age of 26. She became ill in March 1848 and died after a long and painful illness in September of that year, from what appears to have been abdominal cancer and kidney failure. Her parents were devastated, and in John Thomas's diary he gives a touching account of her last hours, and of how after her death, according to her wishes, he filled her coffin with the 'best and sweetest flowers' which he lists as agapanthus, forget-me-nots, sweet peas, mignonette, roses and verbena, and placed a small nosegay in her hand.

It has been suggested that the ghost of Flitwick Manor could be John Thomas Brooks's wife Mary, who was obviously bereft at the death of her much-loved daughter. But although, according to her husband's diary, her health was rather fragile, Mary Brooks lived to be 84, and died in 1879, 31 years after Mary Ann, and it does not seem likely that her grief would have kept her earthbound after so long. Richard Morgan, who is related to the Brooks family, suggested to me that the ghost could even be someone who lived in the Manor before the Brooks family came, or of course, some subsequent occupant after Kate Brooks, the last member of the family to live at Flitwick, died in 1934. However, as he says, the ghost started to appear after the small room in the roof was discovered, and such rooms were usually occupied by servants, so the original impression that the ghost was a housekeeper or servant may be the right one. But if there was some tragedy or sadness connected with a past member of staff, it is not known.

There have always been local stories that the Manor is haunted, and Mr Morgan told me that his mother remembers hearing about a ghostly monk whose regular route was disturbed by reconstruction work in the Manor; but persistent as ghosts so often are, he continued on his usual way regardless and walked straight through the kitchen sink!

The presence of monks is explained by a priory in the village in time gone by, and there is a record of a disagreement in 1283 between David de Flittewic, lord of the Manor, and the prior and two of his monks who were found fishing in the Manor pond without his permission.

Mr Morgan also says that a cousin of his, now 90, recalls that as a child she heard of an exorcism at the Manor, but cannot remember any details. Yet exorcisms do not always have lasting effects, and there is little doubt that Flitwick Manor is haunted today by the lady who leaves a scent of roses behind her. It would be nice to know who she is, and just why she still lingers in this charming old manor house. Perhaps one day we may discover her secret.

2

Message from a Fallen Giant

C ARDINGTON will always be associated with two famous airships, the R100 and the R101, which were built there, and particularly with the R101, which was to perish spectacularly on its maiden flight to India, an ill-fated journey that ended in flames on a French hillside in the early hours of 5th October 1930.

At the time it was the worst disaster in air history, with a heavy loss of life among the passengers and crew, who included Sir Sefton Brancker, the Director of Civil Aviation, Lord Thomson, the Air Minister, and Flight Lieutenant H. Carmichael Irwin, captain of the R101.

And yet on the afternoon of 7th October 1930 a small group of people at the National Laboratory of Psychical Research in London sat listening to a voice which claimed to be the captain of the airship describing the final moments before the fatal crash.

The director of the Laboratory, Harry Price, had invited the famous trance medium, Eileen Garrett, to take part in a seance in an attempt to make contact with Sir Arthur Conan Doyle, who had died three months previously.

Mrs Garrett sat relaxed in a chair, her eyes closed and her breathing becoming deeper. Within minutes she began to speak in the voice of Uvani, her usual control. 'This is Uvani. I give you greeting, friends. Peace be with you, and in your life, and in your household.' He went on: 'I see for the moment I-R-V-I-N-G or I-R-W-I-N. He says he must do something about it ... apologises for coming ... for interfering...'

Suddenly the foreign accent of Uvani changed to an agitated masculine voice, which introduced itself as Irwin, captain of the airship R101: 'Never mind about me, but do for heaven's sake give this to them. The whole bulk of the dirigible was entirely and absolutely too much for her engine capacity. Engines too heavy ... useful lift too small ... gross lift computed badly ... inform control panel ... elevator jammed ... oil pipe plugged...'

The speaker continued, reeling off in quick staccato fashion a full technical account of the huge airship's horrific end only two days before, while Harry Price's secretary, Ethel Beenham, furiously scribbled shorthand as she tried to keep pace with the words pouring from the medium.

The recent disaster with its heavy loss of life had been a great shock to the public. The R101 was intended to enhance Government prestige by a successful maiden flight to India, but problems, mainly overweight, had dogged her from the start.

Today it is difficult to imagine the awe and excitement inspired by airships. Dr Eckener, who constructed the famous Graf Zeppelin, described them as 'fabulous, silvery fish floating quietly in the ocean of air'. They were indeed beautiful in flight, and men dreamed of exploring the world in the greatest comfort in these majestic monsters.

The ill-fated R101 was to shatter that dream. Despite continual setbacks, her designers worked desperately to modify her faults, urged on impatiently by Lord Thomson, the Air Minister. He was anxious to make the maiden flight to India before the end of September so that he could return in triumph by 16th October, in time for an Imperial Conference. 'She is as safe as a house, except for the millionth chance,' he asserted confidently.

Bad weather delayed the R101's trial flight until 1st October, and it was not until the wet, gusty evening of 4th October 1930 that the great airship left her moorings at Cardington, near Bedford. Fifty-four people were on board.

According to eyewitnesses, she got away badly, having to release a great quantity of water ballast in order to soar clear of the mooring tower. She soon encountered heavy rain which dangerously increased her weight, and she flew so low over France that it looked as if she were trying to land.

After passing Beauvais at 2 am the airship dived steeply and crashed, exploding immediately into a raging holocaust of hydrogen flames. Only six of those on board survived, owing to the fact that water from burst water tanks swept them through the flames to safety.

It was a flight that should never have been made, as the voice of Captain Irwin was apparently telling his stunned listeners at the National Laboratory of Psychical Research.

When the press got hold of the story of the seance there was naturally tremendous public interest. Harry Price was a well-known psychic investigator whose adventures in the realms of the supernatural often brought him into the news, and Eileen Garrett was a remarkably gifted medium. But there were many sceptics who found it unbelievable that the spirit of the dead captain of the R101 could return to give an account of the disaster. Was it possible that the medium could somehow have drawn the information from the subconscious minds of those present at the seance? Or had she faked the whole dramatic story after reading about the crash in the newspapers?

Naturally, Harry Price seriously considered these questions, but he knew that the airship disaster had not been mentioned by anyone present that afternoon, and no one there had any technical knowledge of airships. As for Mrs Garrett, she had never even owned a car, and certainly knew nothing at all about aeronautics or engineering.

The stream of technical information which had issued so rapidly from her lips in the voice of 'Irwin' had been taken down verbatim and was later checked by an expert from the Royal Airship Works at Cardington, where the airship had been built. He agreed that it was correct in almost every detail and some of Irwin's statements were also confirmed at the official inquiry into the crash.

Even more remarkably, Irwin had mentioned some scheduled future experiments relating to the make-up of the fuel mixture – confidential details unlikely to be known outside official circles. He also mentioned a German airship, the SL8, which the experts identified only after a search of German records, and used a naval expression that Irwin might have used, as he had formerly been in the Navy. All these facts made any deception by Mrs Garrett seem remote.

Irwin also said: 'We almost scraped the roofs at Achy.' Harry Price consulted French motoring and road maps, looking for the place without success. Even *Baedeker* and the *Michelin Motoring Guide* were no help, but eventually a large-scale railway map of France revealed that Achy was a tiny village on the route to

Beauvais, where the airship finally crashed. Achy would certainly have appeared on the airship's Ordnance flying maps.

There seemed to be no way in which these things could have been known to Eileen Garrett, or to anyone else present at the seance. So was it really Flight Lieutenant Irwin who spoke through the Irish medium at Harry Price's Laboratory on 7th October 1930? And if not, what other explanation could there be?

Eileen Garrett, who died in 1970 at the age of 77, described in her memoirs how she had had several premonitions of an airship disaster. Once she was walking in Hyde Park with her dog when she saw in the sky an airship which slowly vanished. Two years later, she again saw an airship which appeared to be in trouble, with smoke coming out of it before it disappeared in the clouds. She thought there had been a disaster, but there was no report in the press next day. Some time later she again saw an airship obviously on fire, which then vanished.

She realised that these were paranormal sightings, and later, when the R100 and R101 were built, she was sufficiently concerned to warn Sir Sefton Brancker of possible disaster; but he was undeterred and lost his life on the fatal flight.

Eileen Garrett sought all her life to understand how mediumship worked and willingly co-operated in psychic experiments. She came to believe that her spirit controls, such as Uvani, were part of her own subconscious and often insisted that her exceptional psychic powers were no more than 'refinements of the physical senses all men possess', She was never easily impressed by any of the extraordinary happenings which filled her life. 'There may be nothing in it. Nothing at all. Who knows?' she would say.

And indeed, who does? But in a lifetime of outstanding achievements as a medium, the seance in which she apparently made contact with the captain of the crashed R101 airship remained one of the most remarkable.

3

The Witches of Bedfordshire

As I drove along the narrow winding road between Wilden and Ravensden one sunny summer day in 1995, I imagined that it must have looked much the same in 1873 when two ladies had a strange adventure there.

There are fields on either side for most of the way, with a grass verge beside the road, and as Mrs Goodall and her daughter drove along in their pony carriage, they noticed that someone was coming towards them on the verge. She was an eye-catching figure in her long black trailing garments, and both women noticed that she seemed to be gliding rather than walking.

But as she drew alongside, she turned to look at them with an expression of such malevolence that the Goodalls were quite shaken, and afterwards described it as 'fiendish'. The woman's face was coarse and ugly, almost masculine in its features, and as she passed she turned her head, still staring at them with a look of such inexplicable hostility that the two women in the carriage felt drawn to look after her, only to find that the road stretched clear and empty behind them. The strange figure had vanished as if she had never been, although it was daylight and there was nowhere they could see in the immediate vicinity where anyone could have hidden so quickly.

When she made enquiries of local people, Mrs Goodall was told that this stretch of road had the reputation of being haunted, but there seemed to be no story to explain the frightening figure they had seen. Later, the Goodalls were interviewed by a representative of the Society of Psychical Research who was satisfied that they had actually seen an apparition.

It was 100 years later that Andrew Green, the well-known ghost-hunter, was in the area on his way to Bedford one day in 1973, when he decided to stop at a pub. He got chatting to another man there, and in the course of conversation, they got on to the subject of ghosts.

Mr Green was naturally very interested to hear that the other man had had a paranormal experience only the week before, and in broad daylight on the road between Wilden and Ravensden.

'She was an old woman, all in black with a long skirt practically to the ground,' he said. 'She was walking slowly along the path beside the road and as I passed her I gave her a glance. Blimey, if looks could kill, I wouldn't be here, mate. If I believed in witches, she was one. But up till then I didn't believe in ghosts either. Anyway, I turned back and there she was gone, just vanished.'

Naturally this encounter had shaken the man considerably, and as soon as he reached a pub he went in for a stiff drink. When the barman heard about the experience, he commented that the ghost of a witch was known to haunt that area, but he had not heard of any other sightings for some time.

So what inspired the woman in black to patrol her old beat that afternoon? From his remarks, it appears that the man in the pub had no previous experience or interest in the supernatural, and, like Mrs Goodall and her daughter, his encounter with the malevolent, witch-like figure was a totally unexpected and unpleasant event.

It has been suggested that the apparition was Mother Sutton, a notorious Bedfordshire witch who met her death on the gallows when she and her daughter were hung in 1612. She had quarrelled with a local farmer and was alleged to have cast a spell on his pigs with the result that the pig sty suddenly became a mass of hysterical squealing creatures, all fighting and 'rending each other's guts'. This was considered to be sufficient proof of her witchcraft and Mother Sutton paid the ultimate penalty.

In many parts of the country certain areas have names which recall local characters who once lived in the neighbourhood. In Hertfordshire in the woods between Bramfield and Datchworth is the site of Sally Rainbow's Dell. Sally was much feared as a witch, and locals gave her chalk cave there a wide berth. Rumour has it that Dick Turpin took advantage of her reputation and found he could hide there safely when he was being hunted for some crime. Another Sally is recalled in Sally

Deard's Lane at Rabley Heath in Hertfordshire. Villagers believed that Sally's magic allowed her to turn herself into a hare, and perhaps they were right, as after a gamekeeper shot a hare, Sally too came to grief and her witching days were over. The evocative name of Agdell Lane in Harpenden was once the haunt of an old witch, Ann Weatherhead, whose ghost is still reputed to appear there from time to time.

Bedfordshire has Mag Lane, near Hockliffe, on the Hockliffe to Milton Bryan road. This is no place to wander on damp and misty nights, when the ghost of 'Headless Mag' is most likely to put in an appearance. There are conflicting views about the time when Mag occupied a dell there, but locals believe it may have been as recently as the early years of the 20th century.

It is said that at about the witching hour of midnight her ghost in a white shroud rises in a mist from a dell in the manor grounds not far from Mag Lane, and slips silently through the shrubbery to the lane which bears her name.

Sightings are few and far between, but two men walking home one wet night, sharing an umbrella on their way back from the Evershot feast, saw Mag's ghostly figure glide past them, and to their alarm she stopped, turned round and came towards them. As they stood, petrified, she peeped beneath their umbrella. The men hastily dropped it and fled for sanctuary to the nearest cottage, where apparently their hair 'stood bolt upright with fear' and they were almost dumb with terror, but thankful for their escape!

At the north end of Dunstable Downs are five prehistoric round barrows known as the Five Knolls. Ancient skeletons have been excavated there, and people who met their end on the gallows were also buried there in later times. A 17th-century witch is reputed to have practised witchcraft there. Could this be the lady referred to in Arthur Mee's *King's England: Bedfordshire* as the Dunstable witch? She was Elizabeth Pratt, who said she met the Devil on the Downs; he promised her that she should live as well as the best woman in Dunstable, but, alas for Elizabeth, she was duped. Apparently she was incarcerated in Bedford Gaol at the same time as John Bunyan, accused of bewitching several children: two had died and two others caught a strange disease after visiting her. But Elizabeth cheated the hangman by dying before she came to trial.

20

Another 'Dunstable witch', named Sally, was associated with the Priory of St Peter, where the Priory church now stands. Tradition says that Sally, cursing to the last, was burnt at the stake together with her cat and her broomstick. However, at the Priory, the monks soon found that Sally dead was even more trouble than she had been when alive. Ghostly hands boxed their ears, the altar candles burned with an evil green glow, and where Sally's spectral fingers touched the prayer books, the covers were singed.

Something had to be done, and a palmer was called in to exorcise Sally's troublesome spirit. But Sally was not so easily eliminated, and as the palmer began the service intended to rid the Priory of her unwelcome presence, he was struck so forcibly about the head that he fell to the floor of the chancel, cursing her vociferously.

History does not say how he achieved it, but the palmer eventually outwitted Sally by luring her into a bottle, and rammed the cork in tight, with dire warnings that the bottle must never be broken or Sally would escape to wreak vengeance on everyone. The bottle was buried, but since no one knows where, it is said that there were no more burials in the Priory churchyard lest the buried bottle might be accidentally broken and so release the ghost of the evil Dunstable witch.

Fear of witchcraft was widespread in country districts in earlier times, and many people had such a healthy respect for a witch's powers that they dared not refuse her anything she asked for, whether it was food, drink or small sums of money.

Witches were often referred to as 'night hags' or 'folk' and were reputed to get into stables at night and take the horses for a mad gallop until sunrise, when the farmer would find his animals foaming with sweat and exhausted in the stable. It was believed that horses could see 'night hags' even if they had 'turned invisible' to human eyes, and if a horse stopped suddenly in the road and refused to move, this signified that a witch was nearby.

Bedfordshire certainly had its share of such ladies, which is why the stories of their activities are still remembered centuries later.

Sudden Death at Puddlehill

THEY say old soldiers never die, and if the reports of many a shaken eyewitness are to be believed, ancient warriors still sometimes stalk the earth.

Romans, Vikings and Saxons can still be seen by those with eyes to see them. Perhaps they are just a kind of flashback, a visible memory of a time fraught with powerful emotions and action so violent that at the right time and in the right place some unsuspecting passer-by may find it hard to believe his eyes one night as a Roman legion tramps past or some Bronze Age rider keeps pace with his car for a time before fading into an ancient burial mound.

In Mold in Wales it was part of local folklore that the apparition of a warrior in golden armour had been seen disappearing into a barrow there. The barrow which was called Bryn-yr-Ellylon, or the hill of the fairy, was opened in 1832 revealing the skeleton of an exceptionally tall man wearing a cape of bronze overlaid with gold, probably dating back to the Romano-British period. This garment is now in the British Museum.

And at Bottlebrush Down between Sixpenny Handley and Cranborne in Dorset, many witnesses over the years have reported seeing a ghostly horse and rider.

In 1924, Mr R. C. Clay, an archaeologist, was driving past the downs when he noticed a strange horseman galloping alongside. They were no more than 50 yards apart, and he could see that the bare-legged rider wore a long cloak and was waving some kind of weapon above his head. He felt that the figure had the appearance of a late Bronze Age warrior, and watched as horse and rider disappeared into a burial mound.

Long ago, West Mersea in Essex was a Roman settlement and there are stories of the Roman centurion whose marching feet have been heard on Mersea Island.

Bedfordshire too, has warriors of long ago who still take an occasional constitutional. In Puddlehill, just off Chalk Hill, Dunstable, a footpath leading to Houghton Regis was long reputed to be no place for the nervous. The area had an uncanny feel to it, and it was said that from time to time on certain nights, the ghost of a Saxon chieftain in full armour would stalk that narrow path; the effect upon any lone pedestrian can well be imagined.

Those who dismissed such tales as moonshine had reason to think again in the 1950s when members of the local Manshead Archaeological Society came upon the shallow grave of an early Saxon warrior on the highest point of Puddlehill. The cause of death was easy to see. Sudden death had come swiftly from behind when the skull had been smashed by a violent blow above the left ear. He had been an exceptionally tall man: although his grave was 6 feet long, his body had been bent to fit, with his head forced to one side and his spine twisted, the heels of his long legs jammed hard against the end.

It had been a burial in pagan style, with the warrior's shield and spear beside him. Traces of what had been the wooden shield survived, and there were iron rivets and a pointed iron boss, with an iron bar, the shield grip, beneath it. A small knife of the type used by Saxons was also found, and the iron socket of the warrior's spear with traces of wood fibres from the spear shaft lay near his head. Other graves of a later date were found nearby, some containing beads, brooches, buckles and miscellaneous objects.

There seem to have been no recent sightings of the ghostly Saxon warrior on the footpath from Puddlehill to Houghton Regis. All the same, if you do encounter a particularly tall man one night as you walk along that path, and if in the moonlight it looks uncannily as though he could be wearing armour, you'll know who it is, won't you?

Unhappy Ghosts at Woburn Abbey

WOBURN ABBEY is high in popularity in the stately homes league, with its superb house and grounds, safari park and antiques market, and throughout the year millions flock to enjoy its many delights.

It was very different in 1953 when the present Duke, the 13th to inherit the Abbey, returned from South Africa where he had been living to find, in his own words, 'the Abbey in utter chaos, half of it gone and a great gaping crater remaining'.

When the Duke's father, Hastings Russell, had discovered that dry rot had affected part of the Abbey, his remedy in 1949–50 had been to demolish the east wing, a riding school, a real tennis court and a museum. The new Duke found an enormous amount of restoration work still to be done, and death duties of £5 million to be paid.

Rooms were crammed from floor to ceiling with furniture, pictures and china, 'all thrown in anyhow', and the decorative state of the rooms was a daunting prospect, as nothing had been done for 80 years. It took a stout heart and enormous energy to tackle such a gargantuan job. However, the Duke not only decided to have the Abbey ready to open to the public in six months' time, but managed to achieve his goal, the family working with the estate staff almost from dawn to midnight until it was done.

A monastery for Cistercian monks was founded at Woburn in the 12th century, but in the 16th century the abbot fell foul of Henry VIII by recklessly speaking out against the King's divorce and remarriage to Anne Boleyn. Henry was not the man to ignore such temerity, and the unfortunate abbot was hung from an oak tree which still exists in front of the house.

Edward VI gave Woburn to Sir John Russell, later the 1st Earl, in 1547, after he had acted as an executor of Henry VIII's will, but at the time it was a run-down, badly neglected, old monastery, and Sir John, who had several other handsome properties, preferred his manor of Chenies. It did not become the Russell family home until the 4th Earl brought his family of eight children there from London to escape the plague, and it was during his time that the rebuilding of Woburn was begun.

In the 18th century, the 4th Duke filled Woburn with fine furniture, porcelain and handsome objets d'art and many of the paintings and portraits were commissioned, including the beautiful set of pictures by Canaletto.

He created the park where, as Defoe's *Journey Through Great Britain*, 1761 edition, records 'his Grace is now planting every year Giant Quantities of Trees'.

The Russells were a powerful and wealthy family, but the three Dukes before the present Duke were all lonely, unhappy men in their private lives. The 10th Duke and his wife were not on speaking terms for most of their married life. He was succeeded by his brother, Herbrand, the present Duke's grandfather, who had a distinguished public career but a cold, autocratic personality and no desire to make conversation. His wife Mary devoted her time to her small cottage hospital nearby, which is now Maryland, an adult college.

Here she qualified as a theatre sister and radiographer. When the First World War broke out she was determined to play her part, and on 7th September 1914 she wrote in her diary: 'Admitted the first soldiers from Bedford to my Cottage Hospital. I little thought when we built it ten years ago that we should ever see the Red Cross flag flying over it.' During its five and a half years as a military hospital, a total of 2,453 serving soldiers were treated there. The Duchess's other great interest was flying, and her record-breaking flights earned her the name of the Flying Duchess. However, she had to cope with increasing deafness and objected to anyone having to shout, so conversation with her husband was always difficult, and their mealtimes together were silent occasions. Hastings, the present Duke's father, was their only child, but after a disagreement, Hastings and Herbrand did not meet or communicate with each other for 20 years.

There is a room in the Abbey devoted to the memory of the Duke's grandmother, where the pictures illustrate her love of animals and birds, and there is also a model of her plane. She took flying lessons in 1925, and in 1928, now in her early 60s, she and her co-pilot made an attempt to fly to India. They reached Karachi, but it was not a record-breaking trip as she hoped. The next year she and her pilot made the round trip to India and back in eight days, and followed it by a record flight to the Cape. She had several narrow escapes during flights, once making a forced landing in jungle when her plane caught fire and on another occasion being shot at by Berber tribesmen. Her indomitable spirit and adventurous exploits made her a popular figure in the eyes of press and public alike, and flying became for her an enjoyable antidote to her personal problems.

But her deafness was frustrating, and life had become increasingly depressing after her husband had said that her cottage hospital must be given up as it was becoming too expensive. One day in March 1937, when the Fens were flooded, she said she would go to see them and complete her 200 hours of solo flying at the same time. She took off in her Gypsy Moth but by teatime a heavy snowstorm had set in, and she had not returned. A search was organised without success, and six days later parts of her plane were found washed ashore near Great Yarmouth. It seems sad that after her many adventures, an accident so near home should end her life. Or did she decide to take this way out of her unhappiness?

There is an isolated little summer-house on the west side of the park which is not open to the public, and it was here that the Duke's grandmother liked to escape, to be alone with her thoughts, to watch the birds and write her diary. The Duke felt her presence very strongly there, and who can say? Perhaps the spirit of that indomitable and courageous woman does return sometimes to the place she made so much her own.

When Diana Norman visited Woburn Abbey with the clairvoyant Tom Corbett while writing her book *The Stately Ghosts of England* (1963), she said that Corbett felt that some rooms on the top floor were 'soaked in unhappiness over many lifetimes, leaving an overpowering atmosphere of misery strong enough to affect people'.

The present Duke was soon aware of the oppressive atmosphere in some parts of Woburn and of various strange manifestations, such as the phenomena which affected the room used as a television room. The family would be sitting there when suddenly the door would open, although nobody came in. Then, after a pause just long enough for someone to walk the length of the room, the door at the opposite end of the room would open by itself. 'It wasn't frightening or anything, but it would take your mind off the programme, and it could get damned draughty,' said the Duke.

The locks on the doors were changed, but locking the doors made no difference, and eventually that part of the wing was reconstructed so that the old television room became a passage. But the ghost then transferred its attention to opening the communicating doors of the bedrooms, as many guests discovered.

One morning the Duchess found Paul Getty jumping up and down in the corridor where the guest bedrooms were situated. He told her that a woman guest had complained that the doors to her bedroom and dressing room had kept opening in the night and she had had to get up five times to shut them! Paul had suggested that it could have been the heavy tread of the nightwatchman as he walked by which had caused the doors to open, and so he was jumping up and down to see if it was vibration in the corridor which was affecting the doors.

It was not, of course, and the family became used to their ghost's rather irritating fixation with opening doors. But their dogs reacted strongly whenever they sensed a paranormal presence and they would cower and howl miserably. One night the Duchess was walking down a corridor with her dog, and five doors opened one by one in front of her, much to the animal's distress.

She was also rather disconcerted one day when she came upon the Duke and a group from a ghost club in her bathroom. One of the club members solemnly assured her that there were no less than nine ghosts in there, a fact which the Duchess sometimes remembered uneasily as she sat in her bath!

In other rooms in the private quarters the Duke and Duchess noticed a restless, uncomfortable atmosphere difficult to describe, and sometimes they both experienced a sensation as if someone had touched their faces in the night with a wet hand.

It is believed that a manservant to the 7th Duke was killed in the Masquerade Room and his body hidden in a cupboard before being pushed out of the window and thrown in the lake. It is thought to be his ghost which haunts a first-floor corridor.

In view of Woburn's early history, it is not surprising that phantom monks have been seen from time to time, usually accompanied by a sudden cold chill. A cleaner and a workman both saw a ghostly monk walk by during excavation work beneath the Abbey, and in March 1971 a figure wearing a brown habit was seen standing between the entrance pillars to the sculpture gallery, before suddenly vanishing through the door. There have also been a number of occasions when women visitors have felt themselves groped by an invisible hand in the sculpture gallery.

The crypt is used to display beautiful porcelain, silver and gold, but interested as I was on a recent visit, I did not linger as I was conscious of an increasingly strange atmosphere, and was not surprised when I later read that other visitors, staff and workmen have seen a monk-like apparition there.

The antiques centre has its own ghost, a man in a top hat and clothing of another age. There have been several sightings of his tall figure walking through the market, and sometimes lights have been found on after they have been turned off.

The present Duke's son, Lord Tavistock, who now occupies the Abbey, is said to be very dismissive of the family hauntings. But there seems little doubt that Woburn is one stately home where the past mingles with the present. As the Duchess once said: 'Ghosts are quite frequent and most friendly at Woburn. ... When I first came I did not believe in them. Now I have to believe in ghosts.'

The Ghost Who Died for Love

W HEN a beautiful aristocratic young lady falls deeply in love with a handsome young man far below her station, you have all the ingredients of a historical romance that is almost bound to end in tragedy. Possibly if Barbara Cartland had written the story she would have created a happy ending for Lady Elizabeth Grey, but life was not so kind to the lady who now, grey in colour as well as name, continues to haunt the site of her ill-starred love affair.

Silsoe has a picturesque main street with many old and lovely houses; the Old George, a large and handsome inn, has stood here for centuries. Inside it is comfortable and roomy, and time ticks along pleasantly, measured by the many clocks of every size and kind that the landlord, John Bridge, collects.

On the walls there is an arsenal of various guns and firing pieces – pistols, rifles, crossbows and a wicked-looking halberd. Among the pictures and tapestries which decorate the walls, there is a frame containing what appears to be a small purse of leather and metalwork which has been identified as 17th-century. Elaine Bridge, the landlord's wife, told me that her husband found it during redecoration work and she has been told that it would have been the top of a bigger pouch belonging to a gentleman.

There has been another curious find at the Old George. At the end of 1992 when workmen were doing renovations, an old gravestone was found behind the fireplace in the lounge bar. It dated back to the 18th century and the only legible word on its surface was 'widow'. So what was a gravestone doing in the pub? Most likely some long-gone builder found an ancient stone from an old graveyard ideal for his purpose, but this rather gruesome find revived local talk of a ghost.

'People say the place is haunted by a woman,' said landlord John Bridge at the time. 'She is very beautiful and appears grey all over. I have never seen her, but I once felt a strange presence when I went to my bedroom, and residents say they have sometimes heard footsteps.'

The Old George's ghost was a lot more troublesome in 1959; so much so that the then landlady advertised in a publicans' trade journal for 'a layer' to exorcise 'the Silsoe ghost'. Apparently at that time the ghost got up to all kinds of mischievous tricks, and the noise of doors being slammed in the small hours was getting on the landlady's nerves. But when a psychical research group arrived determined to make contact with the Old George's obstreperous phantom, they had no luck at all. The ghost played hard to get, and lay low until they had gone.

After all, in life, Lady Elizabeth Grey had plenty of practice at keeping out of sight while her irate father and his minions scoured the neighbourhood for his headstrong daughter.

Lady Elizabeth was a member of the de Grey family, who were the owners of Wrest House at Silsoe for nearly 700 years. The beautiful Wrest Park was laid out by the 12th Earl, Henry Grey, Queen Anne's chamberlain, inspired by a visit he had made to Versailles. A subsequent Earl de Grey rebuilt the great house and Silsoe church in the 19th century. The church had pews strictly allocated to different farms, others for estate employees and servants, and of course, a much grander family pew for the de Greys, said to be lined handsomely in blue cloth, with Bible and prayer books to match.

So it is easy to imagine that in the eyes of the villagers, Elizabeth, the beautiful daughter of the manor, was a great lady, and no doubt some of them were just as shocked as her infuriated father at what happened. Just how or when Fate decreed that Lady Elizabeth and the handsome young coachman at the Old George should meet each other, and fall passionately in love, is not known. But as for Romeo and Juliet, everything was against such a liaison.

Elizabeth knew that there was no possibility that her father would see her low-born lover as a suitable son-in-law. The only answer was to elope, and she secretly fled Wrest Park to join her coachman at the Old George, where they remained hidden for a fortnight while her father fruitlessly searched the neighbourhood. Somehow they managed to elude him, tucked away in their secret rendezvous, but all too soon Elizabeth heard that their hiding place was discovered and her father was on his way to fetch her home.

The lovers leapt into a coach and set off at a dangerous speed, but skilled as he was, as they hurtled round a curve in the road the young man lost control and the coach plunged into a lake where Lady Elizabeth, helplessly trapped inside, was drowned. What happened to her coachman is not known, but legend has it that his aristocratic sweetheart returned in spirit to the Old George where they had been so happy together.

The Old George was always said to be haunted, and in 1960 a workman had the fright of his life when he looked up to see a grey form pass by. He told the landlord that he had seen the ghost of a young woman in a large picture hat, but he was so impressed by the hat that he did not notice what else she was wearing, other than that it was all grey in colour.

On one wall of the inn is a framed quotation, with no author's name given. It is headed 'Death is Nothing at All', and part of it reads: 'What is death but a negligible accident? Why should I be out of your mind because I am out of your sight? I am but waiting for you for an interval, somewhere very near, just round the corner. All is well.' Remembering Lady Elizabeth, it seems quite apt.

Silsoe has another sad little ghost. An old jobbing gardener called Bill Turner, who died in 1929 aged 96, had the gift of second sight; in fact people said he had one foot in this world, and one in the next. Investigating Bedfordshire ghosts was a lifetime's interest for Bill, and he wrote down his discoveries in an old black leather-bound notebook found among his possessions when he died.

His grandfather was landlord of the Old George at Silsoe, and Bill knew all about the lovely grey lady who haunted it, but did not mention that he ever saw her. It was at Silsoe, however, that he did encounter his first ghost. Not far from the inn was Silsoe House, where Mrs Hallam, a friend of Bill's family, took in lodgers. Bill stayed there one weekend while working on Mrs Hallam's garden, and during the night be heard a tapping noise coming from a nearby bedroom, and the creaking of stairs.

This happened several times and when he felt something touch his hand as it lay outside the bedclothes, he jumped out of bed and lit his lamp. He could hear the floorboards creaking outside his bedroom door, and as he stood there, wondering what to expect, there suddenly appeared a small fair-haired girl wearing a pinafore, but no shoes or stockings. She seemed to be in distress, and ran past Bill, disappearing near the bed.

Next morning at breakfast, another lodger asked 'Who was the little girl I saw on the landing last night? She tapped at my door, and when I answered she just faded away into the shadows of the staircase.'

Mrs Hallam answered: 'Oh, that'd be Sarah. About 30 years ago she lived here with her father and stepmother. The little girl had been looked after by a nurse to whom she was devoted, and when the nurse was dismissed, the little girl pined and died. The man who used to own this house told me that she often appeared in the old days, looking for her nurse. She is quite a family friend now.'

Poor little Sarah, and poor Lady Elizabeth, both lingering in Silsoe where once, long ago, they knew happier days.

I have recently heard of another Bedfordshire pub that, like the Old George at Silsoe, has a resident grey lady. This is the beautiful old Cross Keys at Pulloxhill, only a couple of miles or so as the ghost flies from the Old George.

The landlord Peter Meads who, with his wife Sheila, has recently celebrated 25 years at the Cross Keys, says that their ghost likes to sit in the inglenook fireplace, which can be quite alarming for nervous customers.

'Several customers have seen her,' he says, 'and some won't sit near the fireplace as it makes the hairs on the back of their neck stand on end. One chap must have really upset her. As he sat eating a meal a cast-iron lion above the fireplace dropped onto his plate – even though it was fixed. He was a solicitor – perhaps the Grey Lady doesn't like lawyers.'

Significantly, Peter suggests that the ghost probably has something to do with nearby Wrest Park, once the home of the de Greys. So is it possible that Lady Elizabeth Grey sometimes takes a stroll from her usual haunt at Silsoe to warm her bones by the fire at the Cross Keys? A strange thought, but stranger things have happened.

Was There a Curse on the Alma?

S OME older Luton residents will probably remember the Alma
cinema which dominated the corner of Alma Street and
New Bedford Road where Cresta House stands today.

It was a large, imposing cinema seating 1,664 filmgoers, and
at the opening just before Christmas 1929, a film featuring the
Battle of Trafalgar was shown. This was no doubt especially
chosen to show off the cinema's new Magnascope equipment
which increased the screen from 27 to 40 feet, some 20 years
before anyone had heard of wide screen.

The Alma was lavishly decorated, and above the cinema was
a restaurant with a ladies' orchestra, and a ballroom; before long
a popular feature of the time, a cinema organ, was added, and
an 18-piece orchestra. In the mid-1930s there were Sunday
concerts featuring many radio favourites and later Jack Hylton's
and Harry Roy's popular dance bands performed there.

On top of the splendid frontage of the Alma glittered a huge
globe and the Alma made the national news as the first cinema
to stop an express train! This unlikely event happened because
the red light shining out from the globe was in line with the
signals on the fast up line to the north of Luton LMS railway
station and was mistaken for a stop signal! So the globe light
had to be changed to blue.

Although Luton had several other cinemas, it would seem the
Alma had everything to draw the crowds. However, even before
it was built there were superstitious murmurs that someone had
cursed the site, and the new cinema would never prosper. The
area had previously been occupied by terraced houses and
cottages and in order for the site to be cleared, the tenants had
no choice but to find other accommodation. Obviously some old
inhabitants made no secret of their anger and resentment at this
forced upheaval.

But whether the site was cursed or not, the story gained credence when during construction of the Alma a workman fell to his death from the roof girders into the partially completed circle. Just how it happened was not certain. Some said he had had one beer too many at lunchtime, others that he was accidentally knocked off his balance by a workmate.

Mr Tony Broughall, who lived close to the Alma in those days, used to work there part-time helping in the projection room while still a schoolboy, and later in his teens he became a full-time employee. He told me that some of the staff claimed that the rear of the building was haunted.

'It was certainly a very strange place,' he said. 'People spoke of an uneasy, oppressive atmosphere which pervaded this part of the building from the ground-floor boiler room right up to the projection suite at the top. This whole part was used exclusively by the staff and consisted of a maze of rooms served by two concrete staircases with interconnecting rooms and passages at various levels. Some claimed that when ascending the stairs they felt that some unknown presence was always one flight ahead of them, and when descending they had the even more terrifying feeling of being followed by something which was awaiting the opportunity to push them headlong down the next flight.'

Towards the end of 1943 the Alma went over to twice-nightly variety shows for a time, then alternated film and stage shows, but by the early 1950s its popularity was declining, and to revive its fortunes, it was converted into the Cresta ballroom. But this too seemed doomed to failure after initial popularity, and in 1960 the Alma was demolished to make way for what is now Cresta House.

So was the site cursed, as some old Luton residents believed? Tony Broughall told me that according to the foreman engaged in the demolition work, an old cap, said to be 'heavily encrusted with what could have been bloodstains', was found in the circle girderwork. Did this belong to the unfortunate workman who fell to his death during the construction of the unlucky Alma? Who knows? The Alma is long gone, taking with it its curse and its ghostly atmosphere. Unless someone who works at Cresta House knows otherwise!

Ghosts at the Priory

C HICKSANDS RAF base has been occupied by the Air Ministry since 1939; the United States Air Force also arrived in November 1950, but they have recently left. It seems an unlikely setting for a haunting, but the old Priory building which now forms part of the officers' mess seems to be a strong focus for paranormal activity, and keeps alive the old legend of a ghostly nun said to walk on the 17th of each month, forever searching for her lover.

This story of a forbidden romance in past centuries between a nun and a canon is a familiar one. The discovery by the authorities of her pregnancy brought harsh retribution, and it is said that the canon was beheaded while the nun, walled up to her neck, was forced to watch him die before the wall was sealed up and she too was left to perish.

But did it ever happen? A priory at Cudessand, as it was called then, was founded in the 12th century and became the third largest Gilbertine religious house in the country, housing 55 canons and 120 nuns. But by 1536 when the Dissolution of the Monasteries began, the population of the Priory had been decimated by a succession of disasters and when the prior and prioress surrendered in 1538, there were only 17 nuns and six canons left to be pensioned off.

There is a record that when Chicksands was inspected in 1535 by Dr Richard Layton, he told Cromwell, Henry VIII's Vicar General, that he had found two of the nuns 'not baron', one of them pregnant by a serving man and one by a superior. But there is no way of telling if this is true or not, and since the suppression of small monasteries was in full swing almost immediately after Dr Layton's visit, it seems unlikely that either of the nuns would have suffered the dire retribution the old story suggests.

However, the legend of the walled-up nun gained credence through a plaque in the remaining cloister, dedicated to a nun, Berta Rosata. It reads:

Moribus Ornata Jacet
Hic Bona Berta Rosata

which has been translated as: 'By Virtues guarded and by manners graced, Here alas is fair Rosata placed'.

But when the wall was rebuilt in the 18th century, and again in the early 19th century, no trace of fair Rosata came to light, and when the inscription was examined by a historical expert, he declared that it appeared to be an obvious invention of the late 18th century. 'I can find no medieval use of the Christian name Rosata. It may have been an 18th-century invention for what they believed a medieval name should be,' he went on, suggesting that some member of the Osborn family circle composed the wording on the plaque to add a romantic Gothic touch to Chicksands. I suppose it is also possible that the name Rosata could have been inspired by the name of the founder of the Priory, Rose de Beauchamp of Bedford Castle.

The Osborn family owned Chicksands Priory from 1536 until it was sold to the Government in 1939. Dorothy Osborn is remembered for her long-running love affair in the 17th century with William Temple, conducted over seven years, mainly by letters, many of which have survived and been published. The Civil War which divided many families created a Romeo and Juliet situation for William and Dorothy, as his family were Parliamentarians and her father a prominent Royalist, but her letters were full of humour and day-to-day chat about her life at Chicksands. Yet the story of fair Rosata, which might have been expected to appeal to Dorothy's romantic imagination, was never mentioned.

Just when the haunting of Chicksands began is not clear, but an early reference from the time when the Priory was a family residence mentions that a little girl 'screamed at the lady in black whom she saw in the Blue Drawing Room one day at tea'.

In 1914, a servant who had worked at the Priory for 30 years said: 'I had just taken a glass of hot milk to one of the guests and was coming out of the King James's Room when a tall, fascinating woman dressed in white glided quickly past me. I heard the rustle of her dress and saw the long white train as she flashed by. The time was around 10 o'clock in the evening in winter, and the light was dim.' The witness firmly asserted that she had not been drinking. 'I dropped my tray and fled in terror and told the other servants that I had seen a ghost,' she said. 'I am not sure it was Rosata but I am sure it was something.'

There seem to have been no more recorded sightings until the Second World War, when a practical joke at a party at the Priory caused more of a surprise than expected. An RAF officer covered himself with a sheet and waited outside the King James's Room until one of the girls came up, mischievously intending to give her a fright. She screamed when she saw the 'ghost', who, delighted at the success of his joke, slipped into his room to change. Someone who had heard the blood-curdling scream came up to see what had happened, and also saw a ghost. But this one was a woman dressed in black with dishevelled hair partly obscuring a very old, wrinkled face, who then disappeared straight through the wall!

Another strange sighting happened in the early 1950s when George Inskip, head gardener at the Priory for 30 years, was in the greenhouse tending the ancient grapevines. Through the glass he noticed a 'dark, greyish shape' coming along the path and assumed it was someone coming to see him. But when he went outside there was no one there.

'It was certainly not a shadow,' he said. 'There has always been ghost talk but I never believed it, now I'm not so sure. Whatever I saw was wearing a cowl and came straight up the path. It was dark, and if I had been outside I could have seen it more clearly, but I was looking through the glass of the greenhouse. If it was a ghost I don't know, but I'll never forget it.'

In August 1954, an RAF flight lieutenant came off duty at 10 pm and went to his room to sleep. He woke at 3.45 am and switched on the light, and there at the side of his bed stood a woman. 'She was holding a notepad and was adorned in a dark dress with a lace collar. She had a ruddy face and rather untidy hair,' he said.

Thinking he must be dreaming, he closed his eyes briefly and when he reopened them he saw that the room was illuminated by a strange light, and the woman had moved to the foot of his bed. He closed his eyes again, and fell asleep, but when he woke next morning, he remembered what had happened very clearly and felt sure it had not been a dream. He had heard of the legend of Rosata, but considered that the figure he had seen was not a nun, but a woman in 17th or 18th-century dress.

Another RAF officer, who prided himself on being a complete sceptic about the supernatural, had a really weird experience in March 1957 in the officers' quarters. He was asleep when he was woken by what he described as being 'violently clawed on my left side'.

'Imagine my surprise,' he said, 'when I saw, not a savage apparition, but an intensely illuminated youthful face smiling at me in the most friendly and intimate manner. No sooner had I observed this than it shot away at a terrific speed, receding into a pinpoint of light before disappearing, its going accompanied by a hollow, ringing howl.'

He pulled the bedclothes over his head, his heart pounding and his side feeling quite painful. Then, just in case his extraordinary experience had been some kind of prank, he got up but found his window shutters and door both still firmly closed, and everywhere perfectly quiet. Yet there was more to come, as he then saw the motionless head and shoulders of a middle-aged woman wearing a nun's headdress. She had a serious, thoughtful expression, and was looking past him, and as he watched, she slowly faded. Next morning, he remembered every detail, and any corroboration needed was supplied by the bruises on his side.

A number of USAF personnel experienced odd happenings of a less spectacular nature, and talk of the base being haunted intrigued Sgt Charles Doerrer, so with a friend he decided to do a little ghost-hunting on the night of 17th December 1966.

As they approached the bridge over the waterfall in the grounds at about 11 pm the sergeant's friend grabbed his arm, and said he could see a white, misty figure at the base of a large tree. Sgt Doerrer, who had noticed nothing, dismissed it as ground mist, and led the way onto the narrow footbridge.

But when he looked back, his companion was standing stock still in the middle of the bridge, his face drained of colour and his eyes glazed and staring. There was no response when Doerrer called his name, and the other man's demeanour was so alarming that the sergeant had the impression that he was about to push him over the low rail onto the rocks below.

He hurriedly squeezed by and from the bank once again called to his companion, who this time slowly joined the sergeant. He still seemed dazed and told Doerrer that he felt that he had been possessed by some evil entity that intended him to push the sergeant over the waterfall. He had managed to regain control but after the two men returned to their barracks, Doerrer's friend still behaved strangely, and insisted that something was trying to call him back.

Some days later, when Sgt Doerrer saw his friend again, he said he had been typing when he suddenly felt that he had been taken over again, and when he recovered, he found the word 'ROSATA' typed on the paper.

Another member of the USAF, Harry Cartzendafner, was walking past the Priory at 6 pm on 29th December 1975 when he noticed a figure on the other side of the waterfall. It moved towards the Priory and when it was about 50 feet from him it rose up and floated through a first-floor window. He felt icy-cold and frightened, and for a time tried to avoid the Priory area. But he happened to be cycling past the Priory just after 6 pm one evening towards the end of February 1976 when a cold feeling once again enveloped him, and he was alarmed to see the same figure near a small utility building between the river and the Priory. After a few seconds it faded away.

Harry Cartzendafner said later that the figure appeared to be female, wearing a long, filmy, white robe with a hood, and although he could not see the face clearly enough to determine the age or expression, he felt that her eyes were open and she appeared to be looking at him.

The base is not open to the public but from time to time groups of psychic researchers have been allowed to spend all-night vigils at the Priory. The appearance of lights of various colours and misty shapes sometimes resembling human figures in outline have been seen, and temperature drops have been recorded. At times the sound of singing, like the chanting of male voices, and the chiming of bells have been heard and different witnesses have complained of feeling dizzy and short of breath.

One group who spent the night at the Priory in 1995 encountered a number of manifestations. They saw a misty pair of shadows which appeared to be aware of the watchers, but when approached suddenly disappeared. Later, three balls of white light moved freely around the rooms before disappearing; later still a red light about the size of a tennis ball was seen floating in the upstairs region, and after vanishing from there it was seen by other members of the group moving around the floor below.

After a 20-degree drop in temperature, a misty shape which quickly developed into the figure of a nun in a black habit with a white wimple was seen by several people. Her face seemed to have no features, but was described by witnesses as having an appearance 'similar to interference on a television screen'. The figure, which was within about 4 feet of the watchers, remained for a few minutes before fading.

The paranormal activity at Chicksands Priory seems long-running and remarkably varied. One investigator who has visited the Priory more than 20 times in recent years told me that he saw some kind of manifestation every time. But although sightings of nun-like figures have been reported over the years, there seems no clear evidence of a haunting which links up convincingly with the legend of the fallen nun. Possibly an attempt to make contact with the Priory's ghosts might clarify the situation, but in the meantime, the legend of fair Rosata seems just that: a legend.

Life
with Fred

THERE is plenty of evidence that many ghosts pay little or no attention to subsequent changes in the places they once knew. They pass, unconcerned, through walls where a door used to be in their time, and where floor levels have altered, they may be seen walking along apparently cut off at the knees, or floating on air. But what if the whole building has disappeared and been replaced by a new one? Have the ghosts vanished in a skip along with the old bricks and rubble, or do they just carry on haunting regardless, oblivious of their changed surroundings?

Jill Egerton and her family, who have lived in the small village of Southoe just over the Bedfordshire/Cambridgeshire border for many years, have experienced a variety of paranormal happenings since they moved into their present house. It seems significant that it is built on the site of some old thatched farm cottages, and their ghost, who soon put in an appearance after their arrival, may well be a left-over inhabitant from earlier times.

It was not long after they moved in that Jill had her first intimation that they were not alone in their new home. She woke up one night and to her amazement she could see a figure standing at the end of her bed by the window, apparently reaching up to draw back the bedroom curtains. It was a man dressed in the kind of old-fashioned peasant's smock and hat that farm labourers used to wear, and Jill could see that he was looking at her and laughing, although there was no sound. 'Needless to say I dived back under the bedclothes, and thought I had had a bad dream,' she said.

But before long Jill discovered that it had been no dream. The next hint she had of the presence of 'Fred', as they subsequently called him, was when she was busy making preparations for a special family occasion. It was her grandfather's 80th birthday, and as Jill was arranging food on the table for the party, she felt a hand cheekily stroke her bottom. She turned round, ready to give whoever it was a piece of her mind, but to her surprise there was no one there. And the same thing happened twice more during the course of the evening when there was no mischievous human culprit near enough to blame.

Not surprisingly, remembering the laughing apparition in her bedroom, Jill was beginning to realise that her home was haunted by what appeared to be an unusually light-hearted spook!

Next it was her husband's turn to experience their resident spirit's mischievous sense of humour. Jill's husband had run the water for a bath, and then went back to the bedroom to fetch something. But when he returned to the bathroom he found the bathwater had all disappeared, although the plug was still firmly in place. 'I was in the kitchen at the time, which is directly under the bathroom, and normally any water from the bath can be heard running into the drain outside,' said Jill, 'but I had heard nothing.'

Footsteps when no one was there became quite a common occurrence, and when Jill's son was a child he often said he could hear the sound of feet going up and down the stairs. Jill made light of it so that he would not be frightened. But when he grew up and married, his wife too heard the mysterious footsteps and she will never stay in the house by herself.

One of Fred's favourite tricks is to conjure away all kinds of things, which mysteriously disappear from wherever they have been left. Maddeningly, despite a thorough search, they cannot be found anywhere, but then weeks later they suddenly turn up somewhere unlikely. Jill recalled a time before the central heating had been installed when she put her clean undies for the morning in the airing cupboard overnight so that they would be warm to put on. But when she went to the airing cupboard next morning to fetch them, they were nowhere to be seen. It was weeks before they reappeared, thrown about all over the bedroom floor.

Fred's kleptomania is something the family now take for granted. 'When something goes missing we just say: "Bring that back Fred, we need it," ' says Jill. 'He always does in the end, and we find the missing articles in the most unexpected places.

Sometimes there's no sign of him for months. I don't know where he goes, but he always returns eventually to play tricks on us.'

Obviously, although Fred's little ways may be a bit tiresome at times, he has become accepted as part of the family, and he would certainly be missed if ever he decided to disappear for good.

10

The Bedford Arms Haunting

TODDINGTON is a pleasant village with several interesting old pubs and a manor house with a romantic history. Charles II's illegitimate son, the handsome, ill-fated Duke of Monmouth, came to Toddington with a price on his head. His love affair with the heiress, Lady Henrietta Wentworth of Toddington Manor, is recalled by the Monmouth Oak Tree in the Manor grounds where he and his lover once carved their initials.

After King Charles II's death, Monmouth's ambitions to replace his uncle King James II on the throne received a crushing defeat at the Battle of Sedgemoor in 1685, and his short, adventurous life ended on the scaffold at Tower Hill. His broken-hearted Henrietta died nine months later, and is buried at Toddington.

Monmouth was destined to become a famous ghost, and on the night of 6th July, the anniversary of the battle, people have seen him, cloak flying, riding hell for leather away from the battlefield. I must confess that when I heard that a Cavalier was haunting the old Bedford Arms hostelry in Toddington, and a Cavalier moreover who appeared to have an eye for the girls, I wondered if perhaps the wraith of Charles II's amorous, good-looking son sometimes returned to Toddington. However, when, in the spring of 1996, I investigated the haunting at the Bedford Arms I had reluctantly to dismiss the idea.

The pub is a long, low building in rose-red brick with oak beams outside and in, and it is easy to see that it was once converted from three cottages. At least two of the beams are believed to be ship's timbers. There is a collection of pretty old jugs hanging over the bar, with military prints on the walls, and a handsome scarlet military tunic in a frame. I discovered later that the landlord, Ian McLeod, who died in 1995, used to be in the Scots Guards, and the tunic was his.

The landlady, Gillian McLeod, told me that the pub has had the reputation of being haunted for many years, and pointed out the old brick fireplace in the smaller bar where the ghost has sometimes been seen standing. She was told about it before she and her husband arrived there three years earlier, and explained that there is a tradition that a man who lived there long ago returned home after some time away to find that his wife and child had been murdered. Although he lived there alone for a short time, eventually, unable to bear his grief, he hanged himself from one of the rafters.

Gillian introduced me to Helen Barlow, who works in the pub – a dark-eyed, dark-haired woman who told me that she comes of Romany stock and is the seventh child of a seventh child. In these circumstances I was not surprised to find that she is psychic and well known in the area as a clairvoyant.

That lunchtime the pub was unusually busy, so Helen invited me into the kitchen so that we could talk as she deftly grilled food and tipped large quantities of chips into sizzling fat, producing plate after plate of lunch for the waiting customers as if by magic while answering my questions.

Although some local people think the ghost was a Cavalier, Helen has the impression that he was a seafaring man and she and Gillian usually refer to him as the Captain.

'I sleep here very often,' said Helen, 'and at night he walks down the passage upstairs here. You can hear his footsteps very clearly.'

Helen has seen their supernatural visitor several times, and I asked if he seemed to be aware of her. 'Oh yes,' she answered, 'he's very much aware of what goes on here. He makes his presence felt.'

She explained that she usually sees only his head and shoulders, and described him as a big man with a beard. 'From the way he looks', she said, 'I would say he is probably very shy.'

I asked Helen if she could tell what the ghost was wearing, as this might answer the question of whether he was a soldier or a sailor. 'I have only seen him once when I really took notice of his clothes. He seemed to be wearing something red and blue, a tunic I think, with a sort of elaborate belt,' she replied.

Gillian, the landlady, offered to show me around upstairs; in the passage there she opened a cupboard door and showed me the ancient walls and chimney stack inside. Although the door seemed to fit quite tightly, Gillian said it was always being found open. The doors upstairs often opened of their own accord and this was attributed to the ghost. And she, too, mentioned the footsteps. 'There are no two ways about it, you can hear him walking along the passage here,' she said.

Upstairs in the private quarters there are small rooms with low ceilings and it is easy to imagine the days when the pub was a cottage. Gillian pointed out the doorway from the dining room to the sitting room, saying 'That's where there's a really bad feeling.' The dining room felt warm and comfortable, but when I stood in the sitting room doorway, although it is a delightfully pretty room, I could appreciate what she meant: I could feel cold prickles going down my neck and back and was glad to move away. Was this where the Captain hanged himself, I wondered.

Gillian mentioned a time when Helen saw the ghost in the corner of the sitting room, and said 'Look! There he is, over there', but Gillian could see nothing. Nevertheless, she is conscious of a strange atmosphere at times and says that Ian, her late husband, knew that she was scared of the ghost.

'Oddly enough', she said, 'since Ian died, the Captain doesn't seem to have been around so much.'

Before Ian and Gillian McLeod took over the Bedford Arms, the landlady was Marianne Steele, who was also well aware of the ghost. She saw him standing by the fireplace in the smaller bar, and described him as a Cavalier 'flicking his cloak over his shoulder'.

Apparently, one night the bar bell sounded when there was no one there. 'There were two definite rings on the bell,' said Marianne. But she insisted that she was not frightened when she saw the ghost she had christened Gary! 'I'm not frightened when I see him,' she said; 'it happens so quickly. He doesn't give off any bad feelings, but I don't like to be here on my own. He seems to go for the ladies.'

Barmaid Janet Walker, who has worked at the Bedford Arms for years, has been tapped on the shoulder by the resident spirit. 'At first I thought it was someone messing about, but when I turned around there was no one there,' she said.

There seems no doubt that the Bedford Arms is haunted, but the identity of the ghost seems to be something of a mystery. Is he Gary (!) the Cavalier, or the shy sea captain, or are they one and the same? Either way he seems to be a harmless, friendly entity whom no one really wants to get rid of.

11

Black Magic at Clophill

S TANDING high on the slopes of Deadmans Hill near Clophill in Bedfordshire is the ruined church of St Mary, a place which became notorious in the 1960s and 1970s after a macabre series of events suggested that in this quiet English village the ancient evil rituals of black magic and necromancy were very much alive and still being practised.

One climbs a long, narrow track overhung with trees to reach the ruined church, the gravestones now ranged round the edges of the grassed-over burial ground like a row of watchful grey figures. The ancient church still retains its tower, the nave just a roofless shell with a few strange hieroglyphics scrawled on the inner walls. The site has been tidied up since the days when the churchyard was an overgrown wilderness, its gravestones leaning crazily, but many people still sense an oppressively evil atmosphere in this place where ghoulish vandalism once wreaked havoc.

It was in March 1963 that seven altar tombs in the church-yard of St Mary's were found to have been damaged. Unknown vandals had apparently attempted to dislodge the heavy stone slabs, but found the entrances to six of the tombs sealed by brickwork. Finally they managed to gain entry into the grave of Jenny Humberstone, the young wife of an apothecary, who died in 1770 at the age of 22. The coffin had been broken open and the skeleton removed.

Jenny's bones were discovered in the church arranged in a circle, with a cockerel's feathers scattered nearby. It is said that a child was seen playing with the skull, which had been found impaled on an iron spike.

Was this some kind of grisly hoax? It seemed likely that there was a more sinister explanation such as necromancy, an ancient magical ritual aimed at communicating with the spirits of the dead, and in which a corpse played an essential part. Inevitably the weird happenings at Clophill attracted the attention of the press and television reporters, who were all agog to discover every macabre detail, and to the distress of the parish priest, curious sightseers invaded the village, causing even more damage and desecration to the church and graveyard.

Eric Maple, the writer on ghosts and witchcraft, visited the site on behalf of the Associated Rediffusion programme *This Week* in March 1963. He said afterwards: 'There was an atmosphere I can only describe as absolutely evil and I never wanted to go there again.' A ladder was put into the grave which had been desecrated, and he was expected to make his commentary from the depths 'among the bones'. He was so overcome by the sensations induced by his macabre surroundings that he fainted, to the disgust of the cameramen who were chiefly concerned about the waste of film! 'All the time we were there I had the horrible feeling that something or somebody was watching over us,' Maple said afterwards.

Meanwhile, the vicar had removed poor Jenny's bones to a place of safety; but the vandals apparently returned soon afterwards and finding the skeleton gone, angrily broke up what was left of her coffin and threw the pieces about the church and churchyard. Later on, Jenny's remains were finally reburied in her former grave by the church porch, with 8 tons of earth on top to keep her safe from further desecration.

Six years after these events another tomb was damaged in what appeared to be a similar attempt to remove the body. The vicar bravely kept vigil for a couple of nights, but on the third night when all seemed to be quiet he went home, only to find next day that two more graves had been damaged. And again in 1975 human remains were removed from a tomb and scattered about by unknown vandals. A local newspaper reporter who visited the ruined church at the time discovered a human skull lying on the ground near the damaged tomb, and also a small statuette of the Virgin Mary with the head broken off.

With such a grim history, it is not unreasonable to imagine that Clophill's ruined church and graveyard might well be the haunt of disturbed spirits. One dull, wet November day Mr Tony Broughall and his wife visited the ruins and took photographs. They had the place to themselves, so when the pictures were developed they were surprised to find that one included a figure in white by the south window of the church facing down the nave, and they were unable to find any possible explanation to account for it. On subsequent visits to the site Mr Broughall took a number of photographs from the same position in an attempt to duplicate the original picture, but the mysterious ghostly figure never reappeared on any of them.

'It was all the more puzzling because the floor of the church is at least 6 feet below the bottom of the window,' said Mr Broughall, 'which means that the figure was apparently some 6 feet above ground level.'

It occurred to him later that one possibility could be that the figure was an apparition of a clergyman standing where the pulpit would have been.

Some time later he met a Dunstable schoolmaster who had been allowed by the church authorities to take a small group of senior pupils to undertake a 'dig' in the church interior. They had found a cross bound with reeds buried where the altar formerly stood, and a doll daubed with strange symbols which was buried at the tower end. In the nave they excavated a tomb containing two skeletons, and they also found a coffin nameplate with the name Sophia Mendham, giving the date of death as 1893.

Mr Broughall discovered that some older local inhabitants believed that the ruins were haunted by 'Sophie's ghost'. So had his photograph managed to capture her wraith, or was it some other long-gone resident of Clophill's much disturbed graveyard which appeared so mysteriously on his print?

Even before the ghoulish desecration of St Mary's churchyard in 1963, Clophill had hit the headlines when what became known as the A6 murder was committed in a layby on Deadmans Hill, Clophill, in 1961.

Because of the controversial evidence this case has never been forgotten and several books have been written on the subject, none of which agree that the man who paid the ultimate price for the crime was, in fact, the real murderer.

At around 9 pm on 22nd August 1961 Michael Gregson, a young married man, and his girlfriend, Valerie Storie, were in his Morris Minor in a cornfield at Dorney Reach when a man flourishing a Smith and Weston revolver got into the back seat.

The next few hours must have been a nightmare for the young couple as they were forced to follow an aimless route at the man's direction, until at around 1.30 am he decided he wanted to stop for a nap, and Gregson drew into the layby at the top of Deadmans Hill.

Hopes that there might be a chance of escape if their dangerous passenger fell asleep must have flashed through Gregson and Storie's minds, but after tying Valerie's wrists together the man, without warning, shot Gregson in the back of the head. With Gregson dead, Valerie was raped, then forced to pull his body out of the car, and as she lay on the ground Gregson's murderer fired several times at the terrified girl, seriously injuring her legs. Valerie managed to keep still, and the man, apparently convinced that she too was dead, drove off leaving her badly hurt, to endure the rest of that dreadful night until a passing farm worker found her at about 6.45 am.

The subsequent investigations produced a confused tangle of evidence which implicated two men, Peter Louis Alphon and James Hanratty, both of whom had criminal connections and went under different aliases at times. First Alphon and then Hanratty became the prime suspect as people changed their evidence, Hanratty changed his alibi, and even Valerie Storie changed her description of the murderer. At an identity parade she failed to pick out Alphon, but at another parade, she identified Hanratty by his way of saying 'f' for 'th', as in 'Be quiet, I'm finking', a phrase she had heard him use on the night of the murder. Two ex-convict acquaintances of Hanratty repeated supposed conversations with him which pointed to his guilt, and when his second alibi seemed unsound, he was charged with Gregson's murder.

At the time, Hanratty's 21-day trial was the longest murder trial to be held in Britain, and on 17th February 1962 he was found guilty at Bedford Assizes; he was hanged on 4th April 1962, despite an appeal and a huge petition with 90,000 signatures.

The muddled evidence against Hanratty, some from known criminals, left doubts about his guilt in many minds. Subsequently Alphon privately confessed his guilt to crime reporters, but claimed that the gun had gone off by accident, killing Gregson. He promised to tell all at a press conference in 1971 when a book about the case was launched, but he withdrew at the last moment. Since then there have apparently been no more confessions from Alphon, leaving that nightmare night which ended in murder on Deadmans Hill as yet another mystery in the strange history of the village of Clophill.

Clophill is not far from another much-haunted place, Chicksands Priory, and in the *Bedfordshire Times* of 6th August 1971, an uncanny encounter was reported.

Just after Christmas 1969 a Haynes newsagent, Mr Lawrence Steinmetz, was delivering newspapers to Northfields Farm on the Haynes Church End to Clophill road when he saw a small light approaching. Thinking it was a cyclist, he dipped his headlights and slowed down; he could then see that it was a man on horseback, carrying a lantern.

Mr Steinmetz stopped his car and turned off the lights, and as the rider drew nearer he saw that it was a hooded man 'like a monk'. To his alarm, horse and rider came straight on towards him and rode right through the car.

'My wife and I were terrified,' he said; 'we daren't look behind and I just put my foot down and rushed off. It was a horrible experience.

'We did not mention this to anybody at the time, but about a year later a lady asked us if we had ever met, on our early morning deliveries, a man in a cloak on horseback on the Clophill road. She said she had lived in the house on the hill just before the drive to Northfields Farm, but the family had been so upset by the ghost that they had moved.

'When I told the story to a farmer in Haynes, he produced from his barn a horn lantern exactly like the one our ghost carried, which he said was well over 200 years old.'

Mr Steinmetz thought the ghost was probably on his way to Chicksands Priory. 'The farm drive runs almost parallel to where I believe there used to be a track to the old Priory,' he said.

There can be few places with a fuller history of hauntings than Chicksands Priory.

12

Stand
and Deliver

THE popular image of a highwayman is of a dashing, romantic character in a black cloak and tricorn hat, a roguish smile on his handsome face as he relieves travellers of their valuables, pausing perhaps to kiss the hands of the ladies before disappearing rapidly on his powerful steed. My Staffordshire figurine of the most famous of them all, Dick Turpin, shows him as quite the dandy, with a scarlet stock at his neck and a flowered waistcoat. Such heroes as Dick Turpin, Claude Duval and Tom King are the stuff of legend, and many an inn still claims a reputation as a hide-out for the gentlemen of the High Toby during their frequent flights from the law.

But sooner or later most highwaymen's luck ran out, and their life of crime was cut short at the end of the hangman's rope. In Bedford, the gallows stood in Union Street, and it was there that the highwayman known as Black Tom finally met his nemesis. He had acquired his name because of his swarthy skin and greasy, coal-black hair and when he was buried at the junction of Tavistock Street, Union Street and Clapham Road, it is said that a stake was driven through his heart to prevent his evil spirit from walking abroad.

Obviously Black Tom had inspired fear among the local people during his notorious career, and stake or no stake, to the horror of the local citizens, his ghost began to haunt the neighbourhood of his grave, accompanied by another, unidentified, phantom. In the 1840s this alarming couple were seen several times and nervous people were afraid to venture out at night in case they encountered the terrifying pair.

As recently as 1963 a number of witnesses saw what was believed to be Black Tom in broad daylight. A figure with a blackened face appeared, staggering and lurching along Union Street, his head lolling on one side in a gruesome fashion. As frightened passers-by stared in disbelief at this awful apparition, it faded away and vanished into thin air. This appearance seems to have been Black Tom's swansong, as no sightings have been reported in recent times.

Another villain whose name lived on after his demise was a character known as Galloping Dick. His terrain was the Woburn road near the village of Millbrook, which in those days was the main stagecoach route for Oxford and Cambridge.

Galloping Dick cannot have been too successful at his chosen profession, as he is said to have lived in a tumbledown shack by the sandpit on Millbrook Hill, but he was not forgotten locally, especially on dark moonless nights when the sound of horse's hooves echoed through the village, with never a horse or rider to be seen.

Yet another ill-fated rogue was Jack the Leather, also known as Old Leather Breeches. He met an untimely end on the gibbet on Ivinghoe Beacon after being discovered hiding from the law in some farm stables at Edlesborough.

But there is no doubt that the most famous highwayman of them all was Dick Turpin, whose exploits are remembered far and wide, but especially in the South East. Few ghosts make the national press and news bulletins hundreds of years after their deaths, but in 1948 when a Mr Blaney Key tried to get his rates reduced because he said a house he owned was haunted, the case attracted considerable interest.

The house was Woodfield, in Weathercock Lane, Aspley Guise, said to be built on the site of an older building connected with a macabre story well known in the area. Around 200 years ago this older house was said to be the home of a young girl and her father. She had a secret lover who would visit her when her father was away, but one night he returned unexpectedly, giving the couple barely enough time to hide in a large cupboard in the pantry before he came in.

Unfortunately the father had seen the lovers through the window, knew where they were hiding, and was bent on retribution. There are two versions of what happened next. One says that the father shot his daughter and her lover, the other that he pushed some heavy furniture against the cupboard door, trapping them inside, and heartlessly left them there to die.

However they died, it seems that Dick Turpin took refuge in

the house one day and accidentally discovered the two bodies; he was not slow to realise the potential benefit to himself. He confronted the guilty father, and as the price of his silence it was agreed that Turpin could use the house as a hide-out whenever he wished. The bodies were buried beneath the cellar floor.

Although the original building was eventually replaced by Woodfield, the ghosts of the lovers were said to appear in the present house and garden from time to time. The sound of horse's hooves galloping down the hill was also heard and Turpin's ghost was sometimes seen to enter the grounds, passing through a thick hedge where an entrance used to be.

According to one eyewitness: 'It came round the house, entered the courtyard and faded into the wall of the building. One could distinctly hear the clop of hooves as it passed. It was not an alarming experience, except that Turpin looks a much tougher character than popular fancy supposes.'

In order to consider Blaney Key's allegation that the value of Woodfield had depreciated because of its ghostly reputation, Luton Area Assessment Committee arranged an investigation. Over several weeks, a number of seances were held at the house with two professional mediums, a local councillor, and a number of interested people taking part, including a representative of the Society for Psychical Research and Mr Peter Underwood, participating in one of his first ghost investigations.

Peter Underwood has given a full account of the seances at Woodfield in his book *No Common Task*. Through one of the mediums, the voice of an entity, which appeared to be a distressed girl who called herself Bessie, was heard, but the seances were considered to be inconclusive, and when Mr Key's hearing came up at the Shire Hall, Bedford, the chairman and counsel discussed the matter privately, and the appeal was withdrawn.

A year later, another attempt was made to get the rates assessment on Woodfield reduced on the grounds that the house was still haunted by a ghostly horse and rider, and a phantom white lady.

A girl who had been evacuated to Woodfield during the war was called as a witness and claimed that she had seen the arms of the murdered girl reaching out to her from the wall above her bed. An official asked her what she had eaten that night and when she replied 'Cheese sandwiches', the court rocked with derisive laughter. The appeal was rejected, and the chairman of the Bedfordshire Quarter Sessions Appeals Committee declared the case 'devoid of merit and without point or substance'.

So has Dick Turpin given up thundering down Weathercock Lane, and are the murdered lovers now at peace? It seems likely, as a family living there quite recently commented: 'We know the stories about the house but we have never seen or heard anything ourselves. We do not have sleepless nights over it. I am afraid we are all rather sceptical.'

13

Ghosts
in the Gallery

'So many things have happened here ... but as we have to be here every day we can't let ourselves feel too much.'

Ruth Large, one of the secretaries at the Cecil Higgins Art Gallery and Museum in Bedford, is sensitive to the changing atmospheres in this delightful place, and one Monday in February 1996 when the building was closed to the public, she and her fellow secretary, Jennie Clarke, gave me a conducted tour.

The large Victorian mansion which was the Higgins family home stands in Castle Close, just off Bedford's wide river, and was bequeathed to the town by Cecil Higgins, with his own collection of ceramics and glass, to start a museum. You walk into another age as you step into the mansion, feeling almost an intruder in those richly coloured crowded rooms so evocative of the life of a wealthy Victorian family.

In the library with its dark furniture and wall-to-wall books you almost expect a bewhiskered Higgins paterfamilias to walk in at any moment, and in the guest room with its ornate canopied bed, the visitor's suitcase lies on the floor with clothes in the process of being unpacked by the maid, who has obviously been called away for a moment.

All the rooms have great charm, but my favourite was the nursery with a cosy patchwork quilt on the little bed, freshly ironed clothes draped on the fireguard to air, a splendid rocking horse, delightful old dolls and a small table laid for tea.

Surely, one might think, if there are ghosts they would linger here in the comfortable home they used to know. But oddly enough, it is mostly in the new modern extension built in 1976 that the kind of things have happened that make the staff say 'There is definitely something here.'

The Gallery opened in 1949, and although I do not know exactly when the rather strange atmosphere was first noticed, two attendants who were often there after closing time have recalled the days when the old telephone system was in operation. Very often they would hear the switchboard buzzing as if someone was dialling out, when there was no one else there. There is a small passage leading to a flight of back stairs now blocked off, and when it was quiet in the evening the men would hear mysterious footsteps passing up and down the stairs, and what one of them described as 'hurryings and scurryings'.

'Cold spots' are a familiar feature of hauntings, and the toilets adjoining the Victorian mansion are a good example of how such areas are often quite clearly defined. There is a toilet for the disabled and two ordinary cubicles, and the uncanny atmosphere in the second of these is sometimes so oddly disturbing that none of the girls likes to use it.

'There is a coldness, a feeling of chill,' Ruth told me; 'I don't think it's malevolent, but I don't go in there if I can help it.'

I walked in and was immediately conscious of the difference between one cubicle and the other. There was an extremely oppressive atmosphere that was almost tangible, and I was glad to pass on upstairs to the hexagonal gallery where the staff have heard odd scratching noises that have no obvious explanation. 'I always feel I'm not alone there,' said Ruth. 'It's nothing sinister, in fact, it's almost friendly, but it's quite noticeable.'

We went on to the small costume room, which is thought to have formed part of the Higgins parents' bedroom before the alterations. This is another 'cold spot'; in fact, in spite of a large radiator in perfect working order, the room is always noticeably chilly. Apparently, two workmen were once up in the loft above this room and one of them passed out. When he and his companion came down they were in a state of shock and said they would never go up there again, although they wouldn't explain what had frightened them so much.

Alterations to property often seem to activate ghostly manifestations, and apparently even discussion about changes can do the same. When plans for possible developments in the garden area were being considered some time ago, this sparked off some quite striking paranormal reactions.

'At the time we had two electric typewriters', said Jennie, 'and one day they both started typing on their own. Luckily there was no paper in them! And a few days later the portrait of Cecil

Higgins in the curator's office fell off the wall.'

'Whenever there are changes, something always happens,' added Ruth.

At times the offices have had not just cold spots but strong draughts of cold air with no apparent source. In November 1995 Ruth experienced something even more alarming when she came up in the lift to the upstairs office. As the lift stopped, she could hear what sounded like a fierce gale blowing outside the lift. She couldn't account for the noise and felt afraid to open the lift door, and as there was no one else working up there at the time she took the lift down again and worked in one of the downstairs offices for the rest of the day. On other occasions when she has been alone there she has heard low, murmuring voices from the empty office next door, and sometimes the coat hangers in that room rattle around for no apparent reason.

But one of the most dramatic happenings gave Ruth a real shock. Several times she found the lid of the photocopier open when she had closed it, but one day without warning the machine went completely berserk and the lid and the drawers all flew open with a crash. 'I found it simply astounding' was her comment.

The security alarms have often gone off without cause and the engineers have found nothing to account for it. One morning all the papers on a desk in the corner of one office were found soaking wet, and there was an awful smell there, although workmen found no reason for the crack which had appeared in the ceiling above.

I asked if anyone had seen an apparition, and Ruth told me about the day she was working in the downstairs office at a desk by the window. The back door of the building is just outside the window and absent-mindedly she noticed someone leave; she assumed it was a male colleague. But shortly afterwards when she walked out of her office she encountered the man she thought had just left, and he assured her that neither he nor anyone else had gone out in the past half-hour.

When Ruth thought about this puzzling event she realised that there had been something unusual about the man who came out of the door. He had worn a bowler hat, carried a walking stick, and was wearing smart, old-fashioned clothes more in keeping with the 1930s! 'That was the only time I've seen anyone like that,' said Ruth.

This was a family home until the 1930s, a time when gentlemen dressed much more formally. So did Ruth see a ghost?

In the general office where Jennie and her colleague Mickie work there was another odd incident one day. Ruth had been working at her colleague's desk by the window, and had left the office for a few minutes when the top half of the sash window was mysteriously broken. They found nothing on the floor, such as a large stone which might have been thrown through the window, and it is quite a long way from the ground for anyone to reach up. 'The glass wasn't shattered as you might expect,' said Jennie. 'There was just a really weird hole, shaped like a letter C!'

This is just one more bizarre incident to add to the list of rather strange happenings at the Cecil Higgins Art Gallery and Museum. The staff have noticed that people working there never feel really well – there are headaches, migraines, and so on. Oddly enough, I developed quite a bad headache while we were talking over coffee in the downstairs office. But soon after I moved out of the room, I realised the headache had disappeared as quickly as it had come!

The former curator, Halina Graham, wondered some years ago whether the odd happenings might have something to do with underground water, and invited a dowser to investigate. The dowser suspended her pendulum over a map of the site and spoke of breaks in the protective circle around the mound of Bedford Castle caused by past excavations, through which the earth's energies were escaping. Then, after locating them outside with her divining rod, she used tiny chips of amethyst crystal to 'heal the breaks'.

But something is still disturbing the peace of the Cecil Higgins Gallery. Could it be one of the Higgins family making a return visit to their old home?

Or is it something older, perhaps much older? The Gallery is by the mound where Bedford Castle once stood. This is an ancient site with a turbulent history, and in 1216 the Castle was captured from William de Beauchamp by Fawkes de Breautè, a French soldier of fortune allied to King John. By 1224, now immensely powerful, Fawkes had become a hated tyrant and murderer, and King John's successor, Henry III, came to Bedford to overpower Fawkes and his men and destroy the Castle.

With huge stone-throwing catapults battering the walls, miners removing the foundations, and archers firing volleys of arrows into the interior, the Castle's days were numbered. The garrison surrendered on 14th August 1224 and 80 of the defenders were hanged. Legend has it that if you stand on the Castle mound at night, you may hear the creaking of the gallows!

Today you are more likely to hear the happy chatter of school children arriving for all kinds of interesting activities. The Gallery has so many beautiful things to enjoy that it is hard to leave. Small wonder, then, that ghosts of the past may sometimes linger too, even if the staff would rather they didn't!

14

The Little Blue Man at Studham

S TUDHAM is a pleasant little village beside a common, at the end of which a footpath leads to a small overgrown area surrounded by bushes and trees, near to the school. They call it the Dell, and when I have been there it seemed to me that this rather claustrophobic little valley full of bracken and gorse bushes has a still, slightly strange atmosphere, as if anything could happen. And one day, apparently, it did!

The unusual events of 28th January 1967 began dramatically enough with a single flash of lightning, and the rumble of thunder. It had been raining, and when it stopped seven boys were in the Dell on their way back to school after lunch at about 1.45 pm. One boy, Alex Butler, aged 10, was a little ahead of the others, and he was standing on top of the surrounding bank overlooking the centre of the Dell when to his surprise he noticed 'a little blue man with a tall hat and a beard' standing quite still at the foot of the opposite bank.

For a moment or two Alex stared at this unfamiliar stranger, and then he shouted to summon his friends who came running; like Alex, they too stared in amazement at the unusual sight. Then with one accord they ran down the bank towards the odd little character who stood immobile not more than 20 yards away. At this point a strange whirling cloud of yellowish-blue mist was discharged towards the boys, and the little man disappeared.

Undaunted, the boys began to search for him, running through the Dell and up the bank, and suddenly there he was again, further along the bank. As before, he was about 20 yards away from them, standing quite still, and as the boys came closer, he disappeared again.

When the boys reached the place where the little man had been there was no trace of him, but as their eyes scanned the Dell in search of the elusive little creature, they spotted him down at the bottom of the Dell, not far from where Alex had first seen him. And then something else rather curious and inexplicable happened.

As they stared down at the little figure standing as immobile as before, they heard something they afterwards described as 'voices not like a human'. The sound was more like a continuous, deep, 'foreign-sounding' babble of noise which stopped the boys in their tracks. Were there perhaps more little men hidden somewhere in the bushes who were communicating with the first one? The curious murmur of sound seemed to be coming from somewhere closer to them than the little man, and cautiously the boys circled the Dell, looking down to where he stood, still in the same place, and still apparently rigid and unmoving.

As they hesitated, uncertain what to do next, they heard the sound of their teacher's whistle from Studham Primary School, and the boys hurried off, brimming over with excitement, to tell Miss Newcomb about their extraordinary experience.

It is to Miss Newcomb's credit that after listening to what seven of her pupils had got to say, far from dismissing their unusual story as nonsense, she made them all write down in their own words what had happened, making sure that there was no collusion. After tidy copies had been made, they were pasted in a special book entitled 'The Little Blue Man on Studham Common'.

So what did that group of 10 and 11-year-old friends see that winter afternoon? A little man in blue with a black belt and a tall hat and beard sounds uncommonly like Noddy's friend, Big Ears. Although the Dell is not far from a row of houses and the school, it is quite a wild area. Could it possibly be that with the clear eyes of childhood the boys had seen some kind of nature spirit, or even a brownie in the Enid Blyton mould?

A reader of *Flying Saucer Review* saw a short reference to 'a little blue man at Studham' in the *Dunstable Gazette* of 3rd March 1967. It contained the remarkable information that the boys had seen a blue man, with blue clothes and blue hair. One child described him as 'blue all over his body, with big ears [!], a funny nose and shageu [shaggy] blue hair. I and my friends were startled, he was horrid.' Despite the big ears, one begins to realise that this strange entity was unlikely to be the kind to feature in any Enid Blyton story.

The magazine was contacted and three people from *Flying Saucer Review* visited Studham to meet the boys and their teacher. After seeing the places where the little blue man had appeared, they were able to go into more detail with the children.

During their four brief encounters with the little blue man, the boys' sharp eyes had missed little. They agreed that he was about 3 feet high, with a tall hat or helmet with a rounded top like a brimless bowler which added another 2 feet to his height. His blue colour was more of a dim greyish-blue glow, and he had two round eyes, a kind of flat triangle in place of a nose, and he was wearing a one-piece garment with a broad black belt which had a black box on the front about 6 inches square.

The little man's arms were short and remained straight down at his sides, but his legs and feet were misty and hard to discern. The boys described him as having a beard, and when questioned they said that it divided below the chin and ran down both sides of his chest. The idea that this could have been some kind of breathing apparatus was suggested and the boys agreed that this was possible, but they had not been able to see it clearly enough to know, and this thought had not occurred to them at the time.

The boys had been remarkably observant and made no attempt to embroider the facts as they saw them; their teacher, and everyone else who heard their story, had no doubt that they were speaking the truth, and that this unusual incident really happened.

As far as I know, nothing else emerged then or has done since to explain this intriguing encounter. Could the blue man have been an alien? Or a robot? Was the black box on his belt used to send out the cloud of mist to hide his tracks so that he could evade his eager pursuers by hiding in the bushes? Or did he really disappear when he played his game of hide and seek with the boys? And where were the strange voices coming from? Possibly the black box was a receiver. Was there some kind of UFO parked conveniently nearby? Certainly no one reported seeing anything of the kind.

I'm afraid the little blue man on Studham Common must remain a mystery. But one thing I am sure of: it wasn't Big Ears!

15

Haunted
Pub Crawl

M ANY pubs have a long history stretching back to the old coaching days and beyond, and as centres of local life for centuries it is not surprising that some hostelries should have a wealth of stories of times gone by and of colourful characters who are still remembered.

In some cases the past may seem closer than is entirely comfortable, and throughout the country you will find haunted inns where romantic grey ladies, serving wenches, priests, highwaymen, witches, Cavaliers, murder victims and monks put in an appearance from time to time; particularly monks, who figure prominently in the folklore of the pubs of the British Isles.

One phantom monk even made the East Anglia television news towards the end of 1995, when his unexpected appearance on a photograph naturally caused a great deal of interest. Ghosts are notoriously shy of having their pictures taken, and many a so-called ghost photograph owes more than a little to the photographer's art. A famous photograph of the Brown Lady of Raynham Hall in Norfolk taken in 1936 is believed to be genuine. Pictures of the interior of the building were being taken professionally for *Country Life* magazine when a shadowy form was seen coming down the stairs. The photographer quickly took another shot, and when the photograph was developed, a transparent, misty female figure appeared.

Another mysterious photograph was produced when two visitors from Canada were at Greenwich National Maritime Museum in 1966. They took a photograph of the Tulip staircase in the Queen's House and when it was developed, there appeared to be a faint outline of a monk-like figure with its hand on the stair rail, and an even fainter second figure. There seems to have been no question of fraud, but it has been suggested that someone unnoticed by the visitors hurried up the staircase as the photograph was being taken, producing a blurred image which could be mistaken for ghostly figures. It seems unlikely that anything more will ever be known.

The Kings Arms pub at Newport Pagnell on the borders of Buckinghamshire and Bedfordshire has long had a reputation for being haunted, but ghosts were far from his mind when the landlord, Graham Dodds, asked a local photographer, Peter Cole, to take a picture of the new menu board he had installed above the bar. When the picture was developed, it showed Graham smiling behind the counter, obviously quite oblivious of the spectral figure of a monk standing at the end of the bar, with hand outstretched. It was a surprise to the photographer too. 'I am cynical about these things but this image is unexplained,' he said.

So what was a ghostly monk doing in the pub? The Kings Arms is close to Tickford Bridge, the oldest iron bridge in the country, and probably in the world. Tickford, on the edge of Newport Pagnell, was once a village, where the lord of the manor, Fulk Pagnell, gave land on which a small priory was founded in the 12th century, close to where the pub now stands. However, the priory soon achieved a scandalous reputation and towards the end of the 13th century, the prior was deposed for 'waste of goods, evil living and homicide'! It was just as bad in 1340 when the vicar of Newport Pagnell was beaten up and his house vandalised by the exotically named prior, Fulk de Champagne and a couple of companions. Soon after 1524, when certain religious houses were suppressed, Tickford Priory was among them and the last prior was pensioned off.

So it is not impossible that a medieval monk may still be lingering around the Kings Arms. Soon after the photograph was taken, Graham the landlord was sitting upstairs when he noticed a shadowy figure passing along the wall. And, he added, 'At other times I've caught sight of something white moving around out of the corner of my eye, but when I turn it's gone.'

When I visited the Kings Arms in the spring of 1996, I found that Graham Dodds had moved to another pub, but I talked to him later and he told me of two other incidents which happened while he was at the Kings Arms.

He said that one day when a friend drove into the car park she noticed that someone appeared to be in the office upstairs.

But when she came into the bar she was surprised to find Graham there and remarked: 'You got down the stairs very quickly.' Graham had been in the bar for some time, so he went upstairs to check if there was some intruder in the office. But he found the office door locked as he had left it, and no one there.

The same thing happened about three months later. When the same friend came into the car park she noticed that the light was on in the office, but Graham was downstairs. He went upstairs and found that although the office was locked and no one was there, the lights had mysteriously been switched on.

Kevin and Julie Savage had been managing the Kings Arms for about three months when I called, and although they had been told about the haunting, they had seen nothing of the spectral monk. They have two German Shepherd dogs which seem to have settled down quite happily, but they have noticed something odd about their behaviour. Sometimes the two dogs walk towards the pool table and then stand stock still, apparently staring at something that isn't there.

Julie said that one night after closing time, when Kevin had taken the dogs for a walk, she noticed what seemed to be a misty shape, but soon realised it was her own cigarette smoke!

The pub is due to be refurbished soon. An upheaval of this kind often seems to disturb any resident spook, so maybe the Kings Arms hasn't seen the last of its mysterious monk.

The Chequers Inn at Wootton is an ancient coaching inn with a rather grim story of a groomsman who came to grief under the wheels of a coach and literally lost his head. His ghost is assumed to be responsible for glasses which mysteriously leave the shelves and fall to the floor without breaking. The haunting seems to have quietened down over the years, as in time gone by the Chequers was reputed to have a poltergeist who flung bottles about in the middle of the night.

But landlords Eddie and Brenda Finch think they may have more than one supernatural guest, as bar staff have often complained about the mysterious vanishing customer! 'You see someone out of the corner of your eye in the snack bar, but when you get there it's empty,' says Brenda. 'It seems he comes through what was an old entrance, where now there is none. Nearly all of our bar staff have been caught out by him over the years – but he never stops long enough to enjoy a pint!'

Years ago the Chequers had a reputation for 'mighty strong ale', and rival gangs from Kempston and Marston sometimes came to blows on a Saturday night. 'You could see some fine fighting down at the Chequers,' remembered an old local. 'There were some real tough guys there!'

Successive tenants at another Chequers, the 16th-century pub at Roxton, soon realised that the pub had a guest who never goes home. Mabel, as they call her, can be quite troublesome, turning off the beer pumps, turning on the taps in the bathroom, and even turning off the water at the mains. A few years ago the *Bedford Record* reported that the then landlord had been troubled by a lot of noise in the night, as if furniture was being moved about. At first he used to go downstairs armed with a cricket bat, convinced that they had a noisy burglar, until he realised that it was just Mabel up to her tricks.

There have been occasional sightings of a white figure in the lounge bar, and also in the next-door cottage. It is thought that the pub was once a private house and the cottage was the servants' quarters, and there is the usual sad story of a young maidservant betrayed by the squire's son who, when she became pregnant, murdered her.

Another ghost who has been rather a nuisance at the Fox and Hounds at Riseley is believed to be a nurse, the victim of another coaching accident. She slipped while crossing the road and was trampled to death by the horses of a passing coach. Her body was taken into the Fox and Hounds where apparently she has remained in spirit. At the pub they have experienced the usual ghostly tricks with the lights, and footsteps and other sounds overhead, including a ghostly cough or two!

The old Sow and Pigs pub at Toddington used to have a rather uncouth ghost who haunted the gents' toilets. Customers got the fright of their lives when a mysterious cloaked figure appeared alongside and gruffly ordered them to 'move over'.

The Royal Oak at Woburn had an invisible chilling presence on the cellar stairs which also busied itself turning off the taps to the beer pumps at night, and even occasionally during opening hours. There was also frequent slamming of doors, and an odd habit of removing flowers from their vases.

Bedford's Kings Arms pub has something which must surely be unique. This old inn by the river has a coffin-shaped trapdoor above the bar said to have been used for moving coffins in the days when the upper room was used as a mortuary.

Landlord Colin Moffitt told me that he and his young son have tried to research the history of the pub, but couldn't discover very much. They believe part of the pub dates back to the 16th century, and part to the 17th century, and it was originally divided, the back being a mortuary.

When I asked about his ghost, he laughed and said 'We've got two!' There was a sighting of the ghost in the cellar in 1994 by an employee of the brewery. He described him as a fairly old man wearing a short-sleeved white shirt.

'This is the one that plays us up,' said Colin. 'He throws buckets around, and turns off the beer taps. When I clean out the barrels I hang the taps up to dry, but later we find them completely taken apart – which is no mean feat, I can tell you. I find them all stripped down and thrown all over the place.'

Although Colin is fairly sceptical about the supernatural, he admits that sometimes when he has been in the cellar there has been a very eerie feeling there.

'The ghost upstairs is quite quiet,' he said. 'I have never seen him, I don't particularly believe in ghosts, but we hear him walking around. Sometimes the dog appears to be barking at nothing, and then we hear footsteps up there – creak, creak, creak on the floorboards!'

One day out of nowhere some old nails were suddenly thrown at a customer. 'There were only two people in the bar at the time,' said Colin, 'and my wife thought it was me playing about. They were the kind of nails that used to be made by blacksmiths years ago, goodness knows where they could have come from.'

These are just some of Bedfordshire's haunted pubs and no doubt there are others. Who knows why Britain's hostelries are such a favourite venue for ghosts, but throughout the country there are hundreds playing host to supernatural customers who simply don't know the meaning of closing time. Yet no one seems to mind too much, and customers – the usual kind – are delighted when their local has an interesting ghostly tradition. It makes the beer taste all the better.

16

Ghosts of the Highways and Byways

A s you drive along the busy A5 road towards Dunstable you will pass the picturesque Packhorse Inn, just on the border between Hertfordshire and Bedfordshire. It is here that many drivers have noticed the figure of a man in white cricketing gear standing by the side of the road, and have idly assumed he has just left the pub.

But for a taxi driver in 1970, a much more frightening experience was in store as early one Sunday morning he passed along this way *en route* to collect a fare. To his alarm 'a figure about 6 feet tall, dressed in white' walked straight out into the road in front of his taxi. 'I braked', he said, 'but I was going too fast and went straight through him.'

Shaken and convinced that he must have hit the man, he got out and went back to look for him, afraid of what he might find. But there was no body on the road, and when he examined his vehicle, it was quite unmarked.

When the taxi driver's experience was reported in the local press other motorists came forward to report their own sightings of what appeared to be a phantom cricketer in the vicinity of the Packhorse Inn. It then transpired that in 1958, when the cricket team of Kenwood Manufacturing Co Ltd was returning from a match at Milton Bryan, the team's vehicle had pulled out to overtake a car, and become involved in a serious crash. Two of the team, Sidney Moulder and Jerry Rycham from Woking, were killed, and three others were injured.

The accident happened at the spot where the mysterious jaywalker in white has been seen since. So next time you pass by the Packhorse Inn, take care, won't you?

Yet another place which appears to have a supernatural hazard for drivers on the M1 is the Toddington turn-off, junction 12. There have been accidents in the vicinity of both the north and south-bound carriageways at this point and the reason appears to be something drivers find difficult to explain to the authorities.

The sudden appearance of a man in dark clothes wandering across their line of vision is reputed to have caused a number of motorists to take urgent avoiding action, their swerve sometimes causing a crash. Afterwards there appears to be no sign of the reckless pedestrian they thought they saw, and many a shaken driver is left wondering whether they were dreaming. After all, nobody with any sense wanders about on the motorway. They could be killed! It is then that the chilling thought occurs – perhaps they were.

If one supposes that a tragedy lies behind many a haunting, then perhaps it is not surprising that there are stories of shadowy figures who stalk country lanes and busy motorways, where some past accident or disaster has happened. Or, more alarmingly, as in those incidents I have mentioned above, a figure may emerge unexpectedly into the path of some startled motorist, appearing too suddenly to be avoided. Others harmlessly walk their old accustomed ways, seemingly unaware of their present-day surroundings.

Monks and nuns feature frequently in ghost stories, but to see the phantom figure of a medieval friar in his hooded gown and sandals, devoutly meditating on his rosary as he walks among the shoppers in a busy street, would cause most people to look twice. And yet if you had been in Allhallows in Bedford in 1979 near to the Midland Bank, you too might well have been one of the many shoppers who saw him. He was coming from the direction of Greyfriars where a priory once stood, possibly on his way to Sainsbury's supermarket!

Yet another monk was seen standing in the road outside Edlesborough church late one night, and a passing motorist drew up and got out of his car to see if he needed help. In the light of his torch he could clearly see the monk in his black habit, but before he could reach him, the figure vanished!

Other manifestations are harder to identify or explain, like the eerie happenings in Houghton Regis. Sundon Road at

Houghton Regis is now a mainly built-up area, but 30 years ago alongside part of it there were fields divided from the road by a thick hedge. In those days Mr Tony Broughall was courting his future wife, Georgina, and often missed the last bus to Luton and had to walk home in the early hours. One clear spring night he had left Georgina's home in Recreation Road and was walking along the virtually unlit Sundon Road towards the junction where the Chequers pub stands, when he noticed a black shape cross the road some distance in front.

He could just see what appeared to be the silhouette of a head and shoulders, so assumed his fellow traveller was on a bicycle, but when he rounded the bend, and the lights from the junction illuminated the road ahead of him, there was no sign of anyone. If the figure was on foot there was only one way it could have disappeared like that, and that was to push through the thick hedge. Tony thought it was odd, but he soon forgot about it.

Then, a week later, he was walking towards the junction again one night when suddenly he was pushed from behind with such considerable force that he almost landed in the muddy ditch at the side of the road. The fact that he neither heard nor saw anything or anyone added to the unpleasant shock.

It was a wet night sometime later when he had another strange experience. As he hurried along the same road he was aware of a curious tuneless whistling somewhere behind him. 'The notes were aimless and jumbled', he recalled, 'and whoever or whatever was producing them seemed in no need to pause to draw breath.'

He looked round but in the darkness he could see nothing, and he instinctively quickened his pace as he saw the welcome lights of the junction ahead. But the uncanny whistling continued, getting nearer all the time, and Tony surrendered to sudden panic and ran the last 100 yards to the comfort of the well-lit junction. 'When I looked back, there was only the patter of the rain to be heard, and nothing to see,' he said.

After these odd experiences Tony decided to catch the last bus home in future, and a few nights later, on the journey, the conductor remarked that his bus was unusually full for the last trip. A teenager sitting near Tony replied that after what had happened to him in Sundon Road, he would certainly be catching the bus in future.

Intrigued, Tony moved to sit beside the youth, who told him that he had been riding his scooter between Recreation Road and the junction one night recently when a black shape about the height of a tall man came out of the hedge right in front of him, causing him to swerve violently. He lost control of his machine and fell off, but when he picked himself up he was amazed to find the road quite empty.

Neither then nor later did Tony Broughall find any explanation for these rather uncanny experiences, but he did hear of another rather different ghostly encounter, not far away from Sundon Road with its mysterious assailant.

Late one night Mr and Mrs Doerrer were walking by the Green at Houghton Regis when they saw a little girl coming towards them. Apart from the lateness of the hour, it was a cold night and the child was barefoot, and wearing what appeared to be a flimsy white party dress.

She seemed quite self-possessed and took no notice of the Doerrers as she passed by and turned into Drury Lane. But it seemed so unusual to them that a child who appeared to be between five and seven years old should be out on her own after midnight, and so unsuitably dressed, that they felt concerned and followed her into Drury Lane. To their surprise there was no sign of the little waif-like creature, and all the houses were in darkness. They searched the lane to no avail, and went on their way puzzled, realising that perhaps the little figure they had seen might not be a child of flesh and blood.

In the late 1970s Mr Broughall was giving a talk to a Ladies' Club and mentioned the story of the little girl; one of his audience told him that the child had been seen many times in Houghton Regis as far back as the late 1930s. It was believed to be the ghost of a little girl who had been returning from Sunday school one afternoon, and had run into the road and been struck by a car.

The phantom hitchhiker is fast becoming as classic a phenomenon in the literature of hauntings as ghostly nuns, grey ladies, or the restless wives of Henry VIII. There are similar stories from many parts of the world in which a driver picks up a hitchhiker who then mysteriously disappears during the course of the journey.

Sometimes there is a sequel in which the driver discovers that his passenger died in an accident at the place where he or she was picked up, occasionally on the anniversary of this happening. In one particularly uncanny version, the hitchhiker was a girl, and noticing that she seemed exceptionally cold and pale, the driver put his jacket round her shoulders. When she was dropped off, the driver realised she still had his coat, and followed her figure as it disappeared in the direction of a nearby house. At the house, a man answered the door, and when the driver explained what had happened, said that his daughter had died in a car accident years before. The father then showed him where she was buried in the cemetery, and the driver found his jacket neatly folded on the young girl's grave!

But in the case of Bedfordshire's phantom hitchhiker there has been no denouement, no story of a previous accident, in fact no subsequent explanation at all of what happened on the night of 12th October 1979 to a carpet fitter named Roy Fulton.

Roy was driving home in his Mini van from a darts match at Leighton Buzzard. It was a dark night with a few fog patches, typical haunting weather, and he was on an unlit stretch of road where Peddars Lane becomes Station Road near the village of Stanbridge, when in his headlights he could see a young man by the roadside, thumbing a lift. Roy pulled up and watched the man walk towards him. He was dark haired, wearing a white shirt and dark trousers, and the only noticeable thing about his appearance was the extreme pallor of his unusually long face.

Otherwise Roy saw nothing abnormal about the hitchhiker, who walked up to the van, opened the door and sat down beside him. Roy asked his passenger where he wanted to go, but the young man simply pointed ahead in the direction of Dunstable and Totternhoe, and off they went.

Roy drove on for a few minutes, his attention on the dark road ahead, then as a friendly gesture to his silent passenger, he turned to offer him a cigarette, only to find 'The bloke had gone!' Naturally startled by this incomprehensible turn of events, Roy slammed on the brakes and looked into the back of the van, but he was alone. He had been travelling at about 40 mph, and even if anyone could have surreptitiously jumped out at that speed, the door light would have been activated when the door was opened.

Roy looked back, but the road stretched dark and empty

behind him. The hitchhiker had vanished as silently as he had come, and faced with this completely baffling situation, Roy suddenly felt very cold and frightened. He drove rapidly to the nearest pub for a stiff drink and was greeted jocularly with the words: 'You look as if you've seen a ghost,' to which Roy wryly replied, 'Yes, I have.'

He then drove on to Dunstable police station where he reported his strange adventure. Although the police found his story distinctly out of the ordinary, they sent a car to check the area, but found nothing.

Roy had hoped that the police might have records of someone else meeting the same hitchhiker, but the Dunstable police obviously saw Roy's encounter as a one-off. The local *Dunstable Gazette* published a 'Night Ride Riddle' piece, and the story also featured in the *Sunday Express*, but no one came forward to say 'It happened to me too', and although a local reporter diligently researched newspaper files for several years back, no accident in the same area was discovered to offer a possible link with Roy's hitchhiking apparition.

Since that foggy night, Roy's story has featured in several books, along with an ever-growing collection of similar happenings throughout the world. To the sceptical they are dismissed as hallucinations, or just a bit of urban folklore not to be taken seriously. But to motorists like Roy Fulton, there is little doubt that their brief encounter with the paranormal was all too uncomfortably real.

17

Phantom Vehicles

I N the annals of ghostlore you can find many a story of strange vehicles on the highways and byways, and even the motorways, of this country. A driver who finds himself sharing some country lane with a picturesque stagecoach or who drives past an old inn just as some ancient carriage and pair draws up may think to himself: 'They must be making a film'.

But if the unlikely vehicle should mysteriously fade away before his eyes, who could blame him if he drives up onto the verge or narrowly misses a ditch? Some unfortunate drivers have not escaped so lightly when they encountered a phantom vehicle of some kind apparently bent on a head-on collision, and have suffered a serious accident in their attempt to swerve out of the way.

Yet ghosts move with the times and so do phantom vehicles, and besides the unexplained stagecoach there are now a number of stories throughout the country involving what appear to be paranormal lorries, buses, cars, and even trams.

Near Coventry a 3-mile stretch of the old A45 near Knightlow Hill became known as a place to avoid. Many drivers were alarmed to see a phantom lorry appear, driving rapidly towards them on the wrong side of the road, and as they desperately tried to avoid a collision, it vanished.

For many years reports of the deadly no. 7 bus regularly seen and heard in Cambridge Gardens, North Kensington, were legion. No bus service operated in this area, but late at night many a frightened motorist would see a double decker bus, its lights blazing, and they would be forced to take desperate action to prevent an imminent collision. Blackpool even has stories of a ghostly tram seen running along the promenade in the early hours!

From Bedfordshire comes what seems to be evidence of a ghost train. In the *Bedfordshire Magazine* for winter 1988, the editor described how a young man had recently taken some photographs in Sewell Cutting, now a nature reserve, on the disused Dunstable–Leighton railway line. Oddly enough, when the film was developed it included a photograph of a good-looking young woman wearing a 1930s-style hat, with a railway carriage window in the background!

The photographer and his family were positive that no such picture had been taken by them, and no one else had used the camera. The photographic laboratory which developed the film was equally sure that a stray print from another film could not possibly have got transferred.

Since ghosts are notoriously shy about having their photographs taken, how did such a picture appear on a film of snapshots featuring what was once a railway line? And who was the attractive young woman in her fashionable hat? Shall we ever know?

One quiet Sunday morning in the spring of 1961 Mr Stanley Prescott of Dunstable was driving with his wife on the Dagnall to Edlesborough road towards the Travellers Rest crossroads when he saw a black Morris saloon car approaching from the opposite direction. To his horror, the car was on the wrong side of the road, and showed no sign of changing direction. 'It came straight at me, and I knew if I didn't take avoiding action I would be killed,' he said. 'My car went through a hedge and into a field.'

To his amazement, his wife hadn't even seen the approaching car, and as there were no other cars on the road, she could not understand what had happened.

'It was uncanny,' said Mr Prescott. 'The whole thing was remarkable, and it frightened me.'

So had he suffered some kind of hallucination? Mr Prescott saw his doctor, who could find nothing wrong with him, and he himself had no doubts about what had happened. 'I definitely saw a car that day. I can still remember the incident vividly. It was an old-type Morris saloon. I have often thought about it since then, and reading of the unexplained incident started me thinking again.'

The 'unexplained incident' he referred to was a fatal car crash which happened in 1965 at the same place where he had had his near miss with the mysterious Morris saloon. Another car had been travelling on the same road on yet another quiet Sunday morning when it suddenly drew over onto the offside of the road, causing it to crash into an oncoming coach with fatal results.

The reason why the driver swerved over into the path of the coach was impossible to discover. As the coroner said at the time, 'It is one of those unsolved mysteries.'

Could it possibly be that he instinctively pulled over to avoid an old Morris coming straight for him on the wrong side of the road, and realised all too late that he had driven straight into the path of a coach? A police spokesman commented: 'This is the first time anyone has suggested that there may be a phantom car on that stretch of road.' But is there?

18

The Restless Huetts of Millbrook

I WENT to Millbrook one day in the brilliant autumn of 1995 in search of a very strange story. Was it possible, I wondered, for two stone statues to haunt a church? Surely not. Yet I could hardly wait to see Millbrook's two Tudor statues, whose uncanny history is featured briefly in the booklet by Andrew Underwood available in the church.

The church of Saint Michael and All Angels stands high above the surrounding countryside with its glorious woodlands and farmland, and in the late October sunshine the trees were a panorama of vivid yellow, scarlet and russet.

Today Millbrook has dwindled in population from the days when the local inhabitants enjoyed annual fairs and feasts, and there were busy mills, shops, a school and a blacksmith's forge. Now, although the church is visible from afar, the way to it is quite hard to find. On Millbrook Hill is the small thatched village hall, and close by a narrow pathway winds steeply upwards under a canopy of branches to the churchyard. Tradition has it that the site of the church was once a place of pagan rituals, later replaced by a Christian edifice, which in turn was succeeded by the present, mainly 15th-century building.

Church history took a turn towards the macabre in 1857 when restoration work became necessary, and a large altar tomb with full-length Tudor figures of William Huett and his wife Mary had to be dismantled, never to be replaced for financial reasons.

Apparently in the village the effigies of William and Mary were known as the Warriors or the Worriers, but whether this was before or after the strange events that followed the tomb's removal is not known. But worried they certainly appear to have been at the undignified way in which they had been disturbed.

The two effigies remained in the church but before long disturbing rumours went round the village that the Huetts were making their feelings known in no uncertain manner. No doubt the villagers were down-to-earth people, ready to ask scornfully what two old stone figures could do. Nevertheless, weird cracks and alarming groans were heard coming from the church, and a mysterious glow was seen when the church should have been dark and silent. What could possibly be going on?

In an attempt to quieten superstitious village gossip, the rector had the two stone effigies moved to the rectory cellar, but this didn't suit the Huetts at all. The moaning and groaning noises went on unabated, much to the alarm of the rector's maid. Nothing would persuade her to go down to the cellar to fetch the coal, and the presence of the statues frightened her so much that at night she pushed her chest of drawers in front of her bedroom door and lay there quaking, half expecting a spectral stone hand to knock for admittance.

Obviously something had to be done, and the rector's remedy was to bury the Huetts in consecrated ground in the churchyard. But even this failed to stop the noises, which continued until the roof of the church was renewed in 1888. This work revealed rotting timbers devastated by death-watch beetle, and some people claimed that this had been the cause of all the ghostly noises. But others would not accept such a prosaic explanation.

The Huetts had not been forgotten as they lay in their churchyard grave, and in 1919 the rector, the Rev H. P. Pollard, thought it was time to resurrect them. But no one was quite sure where they were! Mr Henman of the Bedford Archaeological Society, the Rev P. G. Langdon, and 17 boys from the Bedford Modern School Archaeological Society joined the dig. But all they found was a copper coin and what the local paper referred to as 'vestiges of our rude forefathers'!

Mrs Bunker, an elderly resident whose husband used to be the sexton, was known to have a stone head which her husband had once found when he had been at work in the churchyard. Trying to persuade her to reveal where he had found it was not easy, but at last she stood at the churchyard gate and pointed to the spot. And sure enough, this time the band of archaeologists were lucky, and 2 feet down they uncovered the Huetts, still lying side by side in the ground, William minus his head.

Mrs Lilian Jackson, the churchwarden, showed me a photo-graph taken at the time of the scene, with the digging party grouped proudly around the newly unearthed Huetts.

Persuading Mrs Bunker to give back William's head was the next problem, but after a descendent of the Huett family had been to see her, Mrs Bunker graciously allowed William's head to rejoin his body once more in the church.

After their adventures the Huetts now lie peacefully side by side near the altar. They look sadly battered, William minus an eye and an arm, and cut off at thigh level. He is in armour, with a Tudor ruff. Mary is more complete, with an Elizabethan-style bonnet and gown; the central panel of her skirt was obviously once carved with flowers, but like her face, the surface is now rubbed almost smooth. She has lost her feet and hands, which appear to have been deliberately cut off, and one can see that both heads were once chopped off at the neck, possibly at the time when Cromwell's men did so much damage in churches.

The Huetts lived in a house, long since demolished, on nearby Millbrook Hill. Mary died in 1602, her husband 20 years later, and Robert, one of their two sons, is remembered for his amazing family of 11 sons and four daughters!

Despite the 19th-century disturbances, Millbrook church has a peaceful atmosphere. But Mrs Jackson, whose late husband was churchwarden there before her, told me of an experience he had a few years ago.

He had gone to the church one night and was just leaving the vestry on his way out. He had switched off the light, but had come without a torch to see him to the door, and it was then that he noticed a hooded figure in black up near the altar, passing through the arch to where the lady chapel used to be. As an icy feeling of fear came over him he stood there stock still, unable to move, his hair standing on end, until the monk-like figure disappeared, and then he hurried off home as fast as he could. 'He told me he had seen a ghost,' said Mrs Jackson. 'He had never believed in such things until then.'

It is thought that centuries ago a cell of St Albans Abbey was set up at Millbrook and traces of the monastic buildings where the monks lived were still visible as recently as the 19th century. Perhaps some shadowy trace of those far-off days when monks were a familiar sight around the church is still apparent for those with eyes to see.

Millbrook has other tales of the supernatural, such as that of the spectral knight in his luminous armour and plumed helmet who rides his splendid white horse in nearby Ampthill Great Park close to the ancient site of the Royal Castle of Ampthill.

In 1965 a former policeman on holiday is said to have seen 'a white shape of a man riding a horse' in the Park. No one seems to know the identity of the rider, but as the Knights Templar are believed to have owned land here in the 13th century, there may be a connection.

There is also Millbrook's own highwayman, Galloping Dick, who still galloped unseen through the village long after he met the hangman, and, of course, the fairies who have buried a hoard of gold on Moneypot Hill. And don't forget the black hound of hell which a young Millbrook woman once encountered one dark night as she walked home alone. These legendary hounds have many names throughout the country. Call him Black Shuck, Padfoot, the Galleytrot or whatever, you will know him if you ever meet him, for he is as big as a calf, with red, glowing eyes like carriage lamps. But all black dogs have the same terrifying tradition: to see them is a certain death warrant.

And so it proved for that unfortunate Millbrook inhabitant in the 19th century. She died three days later.

Yes, Millbrook is a delightful place, especially on a bright autumn day, but it has more than its fair share of very strange stories.

19

Sid Mularney's Poltergeist

IN the world of ghosts and hauntings, a poltergeist is one of the most mysterious and frightening manifestations. The arrival of one of these destructive and noisy entities can be sudden and without warning, and their alarming reign of terror can, fortunately, end just as suddenly as it began.

One popular theory often suggested is that poltergeist activity has its source in the unconscious mind of a disturbed or unhappy person, often a teenager, but I have never been able to accept that what is called 'recurrent spontaneous psychokinesis' can be caused solely in this way. I am inclined to believe that an entity, possibly of a fairly primitive kind, may be involved: in order to undertake the mischievous activities usually experienced, it needs the energy that it draws from an emotionally disturbed person, often a young, vital person such as a teenager.

But there are many cases of poltergeist visitations when there is no likely teenager involved, and others where typically noisy, destructive behaviour may be combined with a ghostly apparition. And there is evidence to suggest that a poltergeist may carry on regardless of whether there is anyone else present at the time or not.

There is nothing new about poltergeists. Centuries ago, typical poltergeist phenomena were being experienced, and then the culprits were thought to be imps or goblins. Few people would accept such an explanation today, and even in the 17th century there were sceptics, as Pierre de Loyer wrote in his *Discours, et histoires des spectres* (Paris, 1605):

I will say to Lucian and to his like, as sceptical as he, that there are plenty of houses haunted by these spirits and goblins, which ceaselessly disturb the sleep of those who dwell in them; for now they will stir and overturn the utensils, vessels, tables, boards, dishes, bowls, and now they will draw the water from a well, or make the pulley squeak, the slates and tiles fall from the roof, throw stones, enter chambers, imitate now a cat, now a mouse, now other animals, lift up persons lying asleep in their beds, pull the curtains or coverlets, and perpetrate a thousand tricks. These Folets do not bring any other nuisance than disturbing them, oppressing them, or hindering their sleep; for the household vessels all of which they seem to have smashed and broken, are found the next morning to be intact.

People who have suffered the attentions of what appears to be a poltergeist will recognise the above description. Over the centuries the activities of a poltergeist on the rampage seem to have changed very little, as a Leighton Buzzard resident was to discover some years ago when a little DIY improvement to his place of work produced a violent and totally unexpected reaction.

On Tuesday 28th May 1963, the *Beds and Bucks Observer* carried a headline – 'The Ghost in Sid Mularney's Workshop'. A long account followed, describing the weird happenings a fortnight before at premises in Lake Street, Leighton, where Sid Mularney, a motor-cycle dealer and expert on racing motor cycles, had his workshop.

Apparently Sid had decided to remove a partition, which would give him a lot more room in his workshop. It was quite a simple job but as he surveyed his enlarged working space with satisfaction, he had no inkling that he was about to unleash a mysterious force that would turn his premises into a mad maelstrom of frenzied activity.

The morning after he had removed the partition, Sid arrived for work to find three racing cycles belonging to a local racing driver lying on the floor with their fairings smashed. He was at a loss to imagine how this could have happened, but thought one of the machines might have toppled over, bringing the others down with it.

Then a few days later, Mr Mularney was working on a racing gearbox. It was an urgent repair, and although it was late, he decided he would stay and get the job finished before he went home. It was 3 am before the work was done, and he was just getting ready to leave when something quite startlingly weird happened.

'I felt something rush by me,' he said afterwards. 'I looked round and spanners were flying off hooks on the wall and a tarpaulin that was covering a bike took off and soared into the air.'

It was as if the whole workshop became alive, nuts, bolts and cycle parts flying about as if hurled by some invisible hostile force, and Sid, terrified, instinctively grabbed a hammer to defend himself against what seemed like a frenzied attack from an unknown quarter.

'You would have to see it to believe it,' he said. 'I was scared stiff. I got out of the room as fast as I could and made straight for home. My wife was asleep and I woke her up to tell her about it.'

After what seemed to be a poltergeist had made its alarming début, there were many more unwelcome surprises for Sid Mularney in the days to come. One morning when he arrived he found that a huge box of nuts and bolts 'too heavy for me to lift' had been tipped out all over the floor. At other times petrol tanks were moved around, and various items such as large bolts which Sid claimed he could never mislay, mysteriously went missing.

Obviously whatever was haunting the workshop was busy wreaking plenty of havoc during the midnight hours. The owner of a restaurant next door said she had been woken several times during the night by 'strange bangings and clatterings'.

'I looked out of the window but there was never anything there,' she said. It was her little boy who had been the first member of the family to wake up and hear the noises. 'We thought it was just a child's imagination at first, but we soon changed our minds,' she said. 'The atmosphere round here has become very tense. It's all very odd.'

But after a few weeks the activity quietened down and as so often happens in such cases, things returned to normal in the Lake Street workshop. The local publicity had unearthed a few memories, and one lady recalled a strange, rambling house which previously existed on the site. There used to be a huge cellar under the building, she remembered, which would have stretched back under Mr Mularney's workshop. 'I would never go down there. I was afraid because it was so old and weird,' she said.

The premises had once been used as a basket-making factory

and local tradition has it that a man is said to have hanged himself there. Could the disturbances be due to the suicide's ghost? It seems unlikely, as there had been no talk of haunting before Mr Mularney moved the partition. Obviously it was the workshop alterations that had triggered Sid's uncanny experiences. 'It was all very odd,' was his verdict; 'I would never have believed it if I hadn't seen it.'

Lake Street has changed a great deal since those events, and the haunted workshop was demolished along with other old buildings to make way for subsequent rebuilding and road improvements. As a result, Sid Mularney moved to other premises, where thankfully, there were no more unquiet spirits to throw a spanner in the works.

20

Ghosts Galore!

THERE are many stories of ghosts who cling to the home they once knew, no matter how many subsequent owners come and go. But a ghost who likes the new occupants so much that when they move on elsewhere she decides to go with them must be, in the realms of ghostlore, more than a little unusual.

Some years ago Mike H. bought a derelict old house in Gamlingay, just over the border into Cambridgeshire, and set to work to restore it. It had once been a village tavern dating back to the 18th century and there was a lot to do to make it habitable, so Mike spent all his free time there. But after about three months he noticed something strange. He would glance up from his work from time to time, and see what looked like a shadow passing by the open doorway.

Mike was a practical man, not easily alarmed, and after this had happened several times, he casually remarked to the passing shade, 'If you want to come in and talk, then come in and talk.'

The ghost accepted his invitation, replying in an equally matter-of-fact way, 'I don't know why you're working so hard. Your wife will never come to live here.'

And strangely enough, although Mike paid no attention to this prediction, it so happened that three months before the work on the house was finished, Mike's wife left him.

By now, Mike knew his ghost as Abigail, and she had confided that she had come to work at the tavern in 1720, as an unmarried mother. Hers was a sadly familiar story of betrayal. Her lover had been a gentleman highwayman who had soon made himself scarce when she became pregnant, leaving her to bring up Marcus, her little boy, on her own. She continued working at the tavern as a servant, but when the boy was 11 years old, his errant father arrived and took his son away to give him a better chance in life than he could have with Abigail.

Hysterical with grief, Abigail pleaded with her son's father not to take him, but nothing she could say had any influence on him, and she was left broken-hearted and alone.

Mike too, was now alone, but he moved into his converted cottage as planned, and not long afterwards, Abigail made another prophecy. 'She kept telling me that I would meet someone else, whose name began with G,' said Mike, 'and this person would have a son. She also mentioned that she would be blind in one eye.'

Now that his wife had gone, Mike decided to advertise for a housekeeper, and received 54 replies. To his amazement, the second applicant he saw was a woman called Gillian, who had a young son called Marc. And she was blind in one eye!

Mike was beginning to think that the way in which Abigail's predictions were coming true was more than a little uncanny. Nevertheless Gillian got the job, though Mike was wary of getting involved with her emotionally, as he rather resented the fact that Abigail and her prophecies seemed to have his future all cut and dried. Even so, Abigail proved right again, as after six months Mike and Gillian had fallen in love and decided to marry, and Mike adopted Marc as his son.

It was a curious coincidence that Gillian, like Abigail, should have been a woman on her own with a young son, and that Marc should have almost the same name as Marcus, the child Abigail lost.

'It was like history repeating itself,' said Mike.

'And Marc told us that a lady came to him in the night and said she was going to look after him,' added Gillian.

'We took a thimble we had found that belonged to Abigail to a spiritualist,' Mark went on, 'and he confirmed all Abigail had told us. But he would never come to the house because he said he found Abigail's presence too overwhelming.'

This unusual ghost story continued in a yet more surprising way. After a few years the family decided to move to a small-holding in Wisbech in the Fen country, and when they set off in the removal van, guess who went with them?

'She's here with us now,' Gillian told a local newspaper, 'but she's much quieter than she used to be.'

This seems to be a case of a ghost becoming attached to a person rather than a place, as Abigail is obviously content to remain with Mike and his family wherever they go. And it's nice to know that after 300 years, Abigail's story had a happy ending.

The Phantom Housekeeper

Luton's busy Museum and Art Gallery standing in Wardown Park was once a Victorian gentleman's residence, which came into the possession of the council early in the 20th century. It was used as a military hospital during the First World War, and it was during this period that a grey, ghostly female figure, thought to be a housekeeper, sometimes gave convalescent soldiers and nursing staff a fright. But after it became a museum and art gallery, the building's reputation for being haunted was based mainly on the sound of footsteps on the back stairs. These were heard either early in the morning or in the evening when there was nobody in the vicinity to account for the sound.

Andrew Green, in his book *Our Haunted Kingdom* (published 1973), relates a conversation with the then curator, who told him: 'The romantic story associated with the footsteps is unfortunately untrue. The tale is that the ghost is of a Victorian housemaid who, after an unsuccessful romance, drowned herself in a lake in the grounds. In fact, the lake was not constructed until after the Council had taken over the building.'

The curator admitted that he thought he had sometimes heard the sound of someone on the stairs when there was no one there, but stoutly refused to consider the possibility of anything paranormal.

However, in 1971 two heating engineers were working late one night in the cellar, when they heard footsteps approaching down the steps. They assumed it was just the caretaker, but then one of them looked up to see a woman wearing a long dark dress, with a heavy bunch of keys hanging from her belt. As he watched, the figure turned and went back up the steps and out of view.

When the two workmen found the caretaker having a cup of tea in the kitchen, he assured them that neither he nor anyone else had been down to the cellar, so it was not his footsteps they had heard. But what of the lady with the bunch of household keys? Was she the Victorian housekeeper who used to frighten the nurses and convalescent soldiers in the First World War?

Whoever she was, she seems to have given up patrolling the museum for some time now. When I made enquiries there I was told that there have been no sightings or sound of ghostly footsteps for at least 25 years.

Whispers in the Garden

The Swiss Garden at Old Warden, originally laid out by the 3rd Lord Ongley in the 1820s–30s, takes its name from a 'Swiss Cottage', a summerhouse he had erected there.

The story goes that his lordship had a Swiss mistress who gave birth to his son, but the child died at the age of nine, and his grave in the Swiss Garden was marked by an uninscribed cross. An alternative version has it that Lord Ongley's Swiss fiancée was caught in the garden by a heavy shower of rain, and although she sheltered under a tree, she caught cold and died. The Swiss Cottage was built by Lord Ongley in her memory.

The Shuttleworth family bought the estate and rebuilt the house in 1872, and restored the garden which had become overgrown. There were stories in the locality that voices had been heard in the empty garden, and people claimed to have seen a pretty young lady in grey with golden hair walking there.

As the Shuttleworths' gardeners worked in the Swiss Garden, they too began to hear voices and to sense unseen presences. They realised that while getting the garden back to its former glory they had moved a stone cross, and they hurriedly returned it to its former site, after which there were no more ghostly whispers.

Dead, but She Wouldn't Lie Down

This is not strictly speaking a ghost story, but as far as the unfortunate sexton of Bletsoe village church was concerned, it certainly seemed uncommonly like the resurrection of the dead.

Bletsoe was the home of one of England's great ladies, Margaret Beaufort, a patron of Caxton and founder of two

Cambridge colleges, whose son was to become Henry VII. But it is another wealthy lady with whom we are concerned here, and unfortunately her name is not known. She lived in Bletsoe centuries ago, and after a long illness, she fell into a coma. So deep was her comatose state that her grieving family mourned her death, and she was duly interred in a vault under the church, still wearing a beautiful gold ring she had treasured.

The ring glinting on her cold finger had caught the eye of the village sexton, and soon after the funeral he made a secret nocturnal visit to the vault. All was quiet as he lifted the coffin lid and took hold of the ring, but pull and twist as he might, nothing would budge it. It was firmly fixed on the lady's finger.

Having got so far, the sexton was not going to be thwarted now. He meant to have that ring and he drew out his knife, intending to amputate the finger, but at the first touch something horrendous happened. The shrouded form in the coffin sat bolt upright, causing the terrified sexton to run shrieking from the vault; and he must have kept on running, as that was the last the village was to see of him.

As for the lady, she had only gratitude for the would-be thief who had woken her like Sleeping Beauty, and given her the chance to live on to a ripe old age.

Wicked Sir Rowland Alston

The Alston family lived in Odell for 300 years in their ancestral home on the site of the ancient Odell Castle. They were men of consequence – Members of Parliament, Justices of the Peace and soldiers – and there are many reminders of them in the local church.

One, however, Sir Rowland Alston, was the black sheep of the family. He was depraved and wicked in life, and in death, his ghost was the terror of the neighbourhood. It is said that his apparition walked through walls and even tree trunks in broad daylight, and astride his ghostly black horse he would ride into the hall of his ancestral home, leaving hoofmarks on the flagged floor.

Something had to be done, and an exorcism ceremony was conducted by no fewer than 12 clergymen, each with bell, book and candle, to consign him to a pond on Odell Wold. And it worked, at least for 100 years, although villagers who fearfully passed by Sir Rowland's watery resting place swore that at times you could hear him snoring!

But Odell had not seen the last of Sir Rowland. He emerged one day from the pond, refreshed and ready for another spell of haunting, but apparently the Devil was waiting for him, and set off in hot pursuit as Sir Rowland made for the church. He managed to squeeze in through the keyhole, while the Devil, livid at losing his prey, violently shook the church in his rage, leaving five giant fingermarks on the stone jamb of the porch.

Since then Sir Rowland's haunting is not what it was. Apparently he contents himself with appearing once every 100 years and driving a chariot and pair around his former estate. When, you may ask, is there a chance of catching a glimpse of Odell's evil phantom? I understand we have to wait until 2044, so possibly some of us may not make it!

The Return of Old Cleggie

In an older area of Luton is a terrace of solid Victorian houses, now mostly in commercial use. Until a few years ago one was occupied by the old established printing firm of Clegg and Holden.

One of the firm's founders, Mr Clegg, retired in 1950, and died a few years later. After his death all kinds of strange things happened, culminating in 1975 in an actual sighting of a ghost. A fairly new employee looked up from his work to find himself being watched by 'a slim man, about 50, with a sunken face and wearing a grey suit', a description which older employees recognised as fitting Mr Clegg.

Members of the firm who had often had the uncanny feeling that someone unseen was peering over their shoulder watching them work decided that their resident ghost was simply 'Old Cleggie' still keeping an eye on how things were running at his business, just as he used to do.

Not that all the paranormal activities were benevolent. All kinds of things would annoyingly disappear, such as the key, usually kept handy on top of the clock, which could not be found for months, and finally turned up inside the clock itself. An old circular saw with a foot-pedal drive, stiff from disuse, would often begin to move of its own accord, and employees' coats would be found thrown off their hooks to the other side of the room.

One day someone decided to clean an old mirror which had hung on the wall for years, and no sooner had another employee remarked that Old Cleggie wouldn't like that, than the mirror simply disintegrated before their eyes.

Lights were seen on when the building was empty at night, but investigation revealed that there were no intruders there, and in fact, the electricity was turned off at the mains. Unexplained footsteps were often heard, and once an old rum bottle whizzed across the room in front of startled workers.

As recently as 1989, a director commented in the *Luton News* on the odd things that were still happening, mainly objects going missing and turning up in unusual places. 'The other day we had a steel rule that suddenly disappeared and was later found hidden,' he said.

After the firm closed down I understand that the building was empty for some time, and the present occupants tell me they haven't been troubled by Old Cleggie's activities. It looks as if the old man has really retired at last.

Index